ROUGH DIAMOND

NICOLE YERSHON

THE
NY
COLLECTIVE
TURNING DISRUPTION INTO ADVANTAGE

You will never realise how loved someone is until they are gone.

My Mum gave me the strength and mental toughness to always make progress. She gave me many of the values in this book.

Dedicated to my Mummy, eternally grateful to my Daddy - always loved and therefore grounded by my Family.

TABLE OF CONTENTS

INTRODUCTION

*S*tatistically speaking, at the end of your life, you are most likely to regret that you didn't do more of what you love. You will likely feel as though you spent your professional life getting up, going to the office and living the same day over and over, week after week, year after year, decade after decade. Ironically, it's the same people who wind up regretting not doing more who spend their careers resisting change and shutting down creative ideas. I know, because I spent nearly two decades as a change agent in a large advertising agency.

If you found your way to this book, chances are it's because you have a fire in your belly, a hunger for change, and a belief in the transformative power of disruption. If you found this book, it's probably because you know it's time to shake things up but you're not quite sure how. This book puts you on notice.

You have it within your power to do more and be more. I'm going to give you the tools to start. This is your opportunity to change your destiny, so you are the statistical anomaly - the Rough Diamond - who shines bright, even if unpolished, and savors each day for the opportunity it presents to innovate, connect and disrupt the status quo. As I was doing the research for this book, I asked a lot of fellow travelers on the journey to send me their recollections, of which you will find many in this book. Every one of them are part of this story because they were witnesses to what happened, as well as important contributors to the impact we had.

One of the first people on my Innovation Labs team, who really knows how to lead the charge on innovation summarizes it perfectly:

"Acknowledge that fire in your belly and change the status quo. Yes, there will be challenges in front of you, but if there weren't, someone else would probably already have done it. So, find people who share your passion. Make a plan, or just wing it as a starting point. The worst thing you can do is have a meeting about a meeting about it. Don't wait around, you have got to start somewhere... so Just Fucking Do It..."

- Shannon Vaughan

This book explains how to live with disruption and how that's a good thing. Disruption is a word on everyone's lips right now. The dictionary explains it as the *"disturbance or problem which interrupts an event, activity, or process."*

I find the word disruption particularly useful as it suggests a strong and powerful force. A force that can single handedly wreck a business in days and can screw your life Up if you let it. Or, you can delight in disruption because it creates opportunity and you get to do something new and valuable with it. Therefore, this is a book of learning, my learning through the inevitable disruptions of life.

It's a rough guide - a manifesto for those who want to fly above the ordinary. Yes, it's my story but it applies to everyone I've ever met. It's a book about the inevitable things that happen to us and what we choose to do about them. Some are small and you just take them on board and some are large and blow you off course. You can be defeated by them or you can use them as fuel to fire you up.

Dave Trott, a legend in the world of advertising and a great influence on my life, said of me that I was *"an irresistible force against immovable objects."* His words have been a constant soundtrack to my life but they also describe my mission to help people come to terms with disruption.

My experiences have been no different to millions of others but it's what you do about them - these immovable objects - that can turn things to your advantage.

Choosing To Live With Disruption

Getting to do what you are passionate about is a privilege. But it *can* be done and you can achieve your dreams. There's much been written about how to change your luck or alter your life in this way or that but this book is an actual case study and it charts the detail. It talks about a life of doing and never regretting a thing.

When I hear people talk about regret, they explain it's because they hadn't done more of what they love. It's the cliché of our time - people spending their professional lives getting up, going to the office, and living the same day over and over, week after week, year after year, decade after decade.

All their lives they've been telling themselves *"I'll do that thing eventually,"* or *"Once I've finished that,"* and *"When I'm ready...".* But, they never get to the point where it feels like the right time to just do it.

"Every great dream begins with a dreamer. Always remember, you have within you the strength, the patience, and the passion to reach for the stars to change the world."
- Harriet Tubman

Truth And Transparency

Make no mistake - a journey to fulfilment and independence sounds wonderful but is bloody hard. You have to figure your way through the highs and lows and that takes a kind of strength. I will explain how to develop that strength and how I made it all work by learning to be brutally truthful with myself. As a result, it allowed me to be truthful and clear to others.

There's also a great deal to be gained by being transparent. I discovered that if I could understand myself and be transparent with others then I could keep everything simple. I don't have time to clog up my head with *"what may be"* or *"what might not"*. I don't waste my time imagining what people are thinking they might or might not be going to do. I just wait for what they say, look into their eyes and interpret what that means and then work with that. It may not be always what they want to hear - it very often isn't, but it's true. I can then work with that.

Living in a world full of disruption means that complexity is everywhere and therefore to survive *something* had to remain constant. That something turned out to be me.

Being a constant in a world of change underpins the concept of a Rough Diamond. Something so natural and yet rare but something really clear and uncomplicated. Strong enough to cut through the noise and improve everything around it as a result. A Rough Diamond is continuously hardened by life. Always learning and forever refined for the better by its experiences.

My journey to be a Rough Diamond and nurturing these qualities in others can be traced back to my youth and upbringing.

We Are Family

To say I came from a big family is an understatement. For a start, my mother was one of twelve. The age span of all the siblings defies mathematical logic. The family had nephews that were older than uncles. We could fill a soccer stadium.

We lived in East London and we are proud. Growing up in the East was a massive privilege. Being amongst such an enormous family - all of them, great people.

Each Friday night and every Sunday was a family occasion, a ritual. For me growing up was an education punctuated by unmissable meals and the creation of incredible memories. We all lived within just a few miles of each other. Every one of them was from the real world, they were extremely kind and talked the truth. Open and honest conversations and a feeling of no judgements. Just the demands of always trying to *"do the right thing!"*

I don't regret a second of it. I was lucky. And I still love living out East.

From Intrapreneur To Entrepreneur

As I grew into my journey, I became more and more passionate about the idea of change. It's a big preoccupation for business and a challenge for every individual on the planet.

Change gets called a lot of things these days, two of the more fashionable terms are *"Transformation"* and *"Innovation"*. For me though, it's simply about getting stuff done and making progress while everything and everyone is going crazy around me.

Transformation and innovation are big deals for business and therefore hijacked by consultants and agencies alike. It drives me nuts. Clients worry about (and get totally confused by) these words every single day. Billions of dollars are spent every year trying to achieve them and billions of dollars get wasted because the change doesn't work. The scary part is that the business asks for innovation or transformation and then get cold feet as they see what it sometimes takes.

That's where my experiences became doubly valuable. Disruption entered my own life in some really big ways. I had the benefit of dealing with it personally and as I worked with the biggest and best businesses on Earth. I was very lucky and somehow my attitude and experiences gave me the ability to find a way through. That story really erupted about six years ago.

I will explain how disruption at home and in my career were in fact the making of me. Although at times I wanted to scream, amazing support from family and friends gave me the strength I needed. They showed me a path through, the path that helped me avoid the usual pain.

I've learnt some big words on this journey. As you will read, I wasn't especially comfortable with them to begin with. I like simple words.

Two in particular get explored in real detail - the *"intrapreneur"* and the *"entrepreneur"*. Intrapreneurship is the act of behaving like an entrepreneur while working within a large organization and the *"entrepreneur"* traditionally defined as the process of designing, launching and running a new business, a startup company.

I've been told that a personality like mine is *"entrepreneurial"*. I have accepted it now. I started out as the *"intrapreneur"* and grew into the *"entrepreneur"*. Don't worry I will explain what they mean and how they will help throughout the book.

I know that it's easier sometimes to say no but I rarely do. The entrepreneurial spirit won't accept no. It makes me busier but that's what you need to be to get things done. As they say, if you want something done, ask a busy person. That's me.

I tend to sympathize with people who say they've got too much to work on or it's too much of a pain. But an entrepreneur knows when to say yes and how to deal with it to get it done. An entrepreneur sets the expectation that it will get done. It does.

If it is worth doing, however difficult it feels in terms of logistics, I will always get it done somehow. A doer will always know someone, somewhere, somehow, to make it happen.

The Rough Diamond Toolbox

Disruption is a wonderful teacher. It can be harsh, and it can seem unfair, but it exists and we all have to deal with it. This book puts all these things into context and that's important as each *"tool"* is important and needs to be used at the right moment. You have to notice when that moment is.

A big factor for success in dealing with disruption, and a powerful tool, was the sharpening of my ability to notice. Just notice stuff. I know that may sound simple and perhaps a bit trite, but it is true.

Noticing the small things leads to what many of us call second sight, instinct and even insight. It's uncanny how the smallest narrowing of someone's eye or the increasing regularity of a particular conversation gives us a feeling that something is changing.

I've noticed just how few people notice things.

Developing my *"noticing"* allowed me to know when that big wave was going to hit the beach. Just as the birds and animals disappear way ahead of humans when danger approaches, I've developed an instinct for it.

Noticing enables us to predict and be ready but it's also a big part of how to learn life's lessons. When things have already happened, you notice why something turned out the way it did. It speeds up everything. Encourages us to stay alert, notice the activity, and the emerging trends unfolding all around. It keeps me alive to what's going down. It makes me able to speak about a wide range of topics. People notice.

I'm worried that whole chunks of society have become so disinterested in life, and their role in it. I talk about this in later chapters of the book and continue to do what I can to reach out to more and more people, especially the youth and the startups on this topic.

This book explains how to deal with the expectations of others. How a strong sense of self can work miracles. How telling the truth (no matter how much it hurts) is far better that revising and updating a lie. That doesn't ever make it the truth. Facing up to stuff that hurts and experiencing the truth behind a failure is a powerful thing. I explain how it allows you to quickly move on, to continue moving forward.

I learned that a lot of business life was frustrating and badly managed. It made me restless for change. I'm pretty disinterested with the average. I tell people the truth. It can get me into trouble but most of the time it gets me where I want to go, and fast.

Wasted time is an enemy to me and I find it hard not to tell people what I really feel. Especially when I see them wasting their lives, putting stuff off, or when I think they are wasting my time. I've found that it's vital to live in the moment, who knows what will be happening tomorrow.

There's a Chinese Proverb that states "The Best Time To Plant A Tree Was 20 Years Ago, The Second-Best Time Is Now."

Time is the most precious thing we have. To me, creating value has always been about doing what's needed right now. Doing things in parallel, doing it ahead of being ready and learning while doing. I've always thought that *right now* is the right time.

Too many of us spend our time, and waste our careers, resisting change and letting disruption wash us away. A typical position for many people to take is to shut down all the innovative stuff and stifle creative ideas for fear of its failure. It's like lying down and giving up.

Too many people have developed an extreme stance, putting stuff off *"until later",* through this irrational resistance of the unknown. They default to the idea that each and every innovation becomes a leap into risk.

This book charts a journey - it explains the value of doing versus putting stuff off. This book is designed to help others see that it's entirely possible to get stuff done, right now.

Right Now

The world we now live in has become deeply crazy, noisy and dangerous. It seems we've lost a lot of direction in our personal lives and in business. My journey has taught me that it's important to actually give a damn. To care and to engage and make things different. We can't just sit there and watch what happens. I think people need to care more. Even caring at all, would be a great start for some.

"In the future, there will be three kinds of people, those that make it happen, those that watch what happens and those that wonder what happened..."
–John M Richardson

The culture of business is, all too often, to penalize the risk takers and not applaud their ability to create new opportunities. It's not surprising but it's just never been acceptable to me. I couldn't ever live a life of adherence to stupid rules and abide by incompetent systems. I'm always asking *"why?"*

I need things to make sense in my head and then I can accept it, perhaps! I've never been good with being judged by ignorance, especially from those with little knowledge of a particular situation. I've also never suffered from a lack of confidence or speaking out about the daft stuff. I've learnt that it's this type of acceptance, and the behavior that grows up to defend it, that breeds regret.

My story explains why adversity is just another part of life - to be celebrated by being understood. It uses many references from the brilliant people who I'm proud to call friends. It describes a lot about the ad industry, but frankly the lessons are wholly transferable to every industry. **Spoiler alert: It is all about people, not industries**.

Simon Sinek, author, motivational speaker, and renowned marketing consultant says so powerfully:

"Working hard for something we don't care about is called stress. Working hard for something we love, is called passion."

Rough Diamond And The Irresistible Force

Finding more diamonds.

I will never veer away from being honest. I've found that it marked me out. Some would be uncomfortable but mostly people knew where I stood. I don't stop until it's done. I don't mince words. I let people know what's on my mind. It has allowed me to be open to those who understood. I attracted other doers and those who wanted to make a difference.

The path I took was filled with like minds. Like minds are easy to spot - they are kindred spirits. The others, the disinterested ones continue looking at their phones. The like minds, the interested and curious ones listen with rapt attention, a notebook open, they are scrawling.

The others are worth working on too. And I explain how I get to them and hopefully turn some of them around.

The Starfish Story

One day, a man was walking along the beach and far off in the distance, he saw what looked like someone dancing. But as he drew closer, the man noticed that it was a little girl picking up starfish from the shore and tossing them back into the ocean.

As he approached the girl, he paused for a moment, kind of puzzled, then asked,"Young lady, why are you throwing starfish into the ocean?" And she replied, "Well, the sun is up, and the tide is going out. If I leave these starfish on the beach, the sun will dry them up and they will die."

And the man said, "But there are thousands of starfish washed up all along this beach for miles! You can't possibly make a difference!" The young girl thought for a moment, then slowly leaned over, and carefully picked up another starfish from the sand.

And with the starfish in hand, she turned to the man and gently said, "You may be right, but it'll make a difference to this one!"

In The Beginning There Was A Word… And the Word Was Disruption

Disruption is defined by the huge shifts in our lives and in our experiences of the world. They may also be made up by countless small ones too, but when they tip there are seismic shifts.

My experience in this one industry is applicable to every industry. It is a perfect example of an industry in disruption right now. My experience focused on the rise of technological change and digitization across every sector and the disruption it has caused to all aspects of life, and in every society on Earth.

I hope that by reading this book you will smile and take a deep breath, but above all that, you will see yourself in it and some of my experiences will rub off on you.

Ultimately, this book is about how to live a truthful life without regrets. It's about how to turn the inevitable disruptions into advantages, and in doing so, polish your own diamond.

1

DIRECTING TRAFFIC

*"When Maggie Thatcher said, "If you want something said,
ask a man. If you want something done, ask a woman,"
she was talking about Nicole. We got double the work out of our
creative dept. when Nicole ran it."*
- Dave Trott

I was 19 years old. I was inspired by the advertising on the TV. At the time, there were only two channels that showed advertising. They were known as ITV and Channel 4 in the UK. The ads that were on all the poster sites were hugely inspiring, and I wanted to get into the business.

My Dad had been on the media side of things, but I wanted to go to the creative side of things.

So, I wrote letters to the top 100 agencies of the time. This was the late 80's, and out of 100 written letters, I got maybe 30 responds, 20 thanks but no thanks, 5 *"keep me on records,"* 5 interviews and, thankfully, 1 job at GGT!

When I first got there, I noticed that everyone was scared of Dave. Dave Trott was the Founding Creative Partner of the agency. His role was Executive Creative Director. Dave was, and still is, a legend in the advertising industry.

A small number of creatives were working on many different ads. There was fear mixed with excitement. I discovered it was crucial to do my job without emotion. I saw that the way through was to just use logic. I saw that something needed to get done and we needed to get to the end of it.

I became an expert at understanding and interpreting Dave's personality. This proved extremely important for me to do my job efficiently. I wanted to do a good job for Dave, he was such a great leader within the company and always managed to get the best out of us all. I remember thinking he was very firm but fair. I could deal with that because there was an honesty about it. All these years on, Dave is still a mentor to me. I have always followed his mantra *"simple is smart and complicated is stupid."*

And so, over the years, I started to get to learn the many different personalities and how to get the best out of people. As an example, if Dave was wearing his dark glasses one day it would mean he was tired and couldn't get his lenses in. I would try and get as much done as possible without people going in and irritating him. I learned to get a lot of stuff done this way. At the time, I didn't know it was my introduction to emotional intelligence.

Emotional intelligence, now that was a new expression on me. I thought it was a strange but interesting phrase and went and checked it out. What I discovered made complete sense.

The first thing I found out was that people with average IQs outperform those with the highest IQs seventy percent of the time. Really? That was no news to me. For some reason, to me that was common sense and nothing much to do with intelligence. Back then, people often seemed to assume IQ was the sole source of success. Decades of research now confirm that emotional intelligence (EI) is actually the critical factor. It's what sets rock star performers apart from the rest of the pack.

Emotional intelligence is the intangible bit inside every one of us that means we can relate to what's going on in others. And that's what mattered to me. It affected how I operated most of the time and drove me much more than anything else. It informed how I managed my behavior. It was how I made personal decisions. It was how I showed up socially and in those early years how I got results.

Playing In The Traffic

Within two years, I was running traffic at one of the top agencies in London. Just like a soccer team, if you're a goalie you wouldn't be going up to score goals. I would figure out who did what and who was best at this or that. Understanding people's strengths and getting the best out of them.

Traffic within an agency is like the proverbial cog in a wheel. You simply made sure that things were done on time, didn't go over budget, the right people signed off, the right work came out on time with everyone happy.

It meant I was involved in every facet of the agency's work, not just the creative production but also the media department. All this at age 21!

It was incredible and a pretty glamorous industry. GGT was what was known in the industry as a hot shop. The advertising industry in those days was in high regard as a profession. For those of you who aren't that familiar it went like this: clients, brand owners mostly, would want their product promoted on TV or the big outdoor posters or newspapers, or all of them simultaneously. TV was always the star of the show, so it was high profile and sexy. There was only one channel in the UK in those days, ITV, everybody would watch, and everybody knew.

It was pretty cool to be able to follow a *"job"* through all of that. To see what started as a sketch on a notepad to being filmed and then brought to air. You would see something you had a hand in everywhere and hear everyone talking about it. Everybody would comment, laugh or cringe at the output of the industry so you really cared. Everyone cared and everyone wanted to win the awards. That was a sign that we had done a great job.

Clients wanted to be with the agencies that won the awards. The best talent wanted to play for the best agencies. Just like soccer teams. Clients paid bigger money to the better agencies. The brief was always the critical part of the process. Get that wrong and it was never going to end well. Ideas would be sold in by very smooth account directors and the pressure to get the client to buy the idea was a big part of the art.

Then it went crazy to get what was an artist's impression or a bunch of storyboards turned into a real thing, a TV commercial or something that could be printed. I learned enough intricacies to be dangerous in under a year. In this era, it really was about craft and art. Ideas and copy still are a very particular talent but back then things were literally stuck down with glue and everything visual was - well art. In the early days at GGT, many of the directors of the TV commercials soon became famous Hollywood and British Film Directors, from Ridley and Tony Scott, Lord David Puttnam, Alan Parker and many others. They cut their teeth within the London advertising scene.

You have to remember, there was no digital technology in those days. If you had to get a poster out, you had eight weeks to get the artwork done, copy approved, and then print and post it. With some poor soul having to paste the poster onto a billboard, climbing up on a huge ladder.

Today you would just do a quick upload. Not then.

The Apple Mac was only just coming onto the scene. Everything had to be done by hand. There wasn't the luxury of mistakes where timing was concerned. It was beyond important to make sure things happened on time. I became finely tuned to what you needed to do to get things done. I worked out that some people I would give more time to and some needed a rocket up their backside. It was only by deeply understanding people that you could get all these things to happen.

One day, I had to ask a very senior creative to do some copy on a print ad. We needed it done by 12 o'clock and for Dave to sign it. The creative copywriter was writing scripts & producing TV ads, so he wasn't interested in doing copy for this.

The first time I walked into his office and asked him to do the copy, he told me to *"fuck off."* Dave Trott's presence was weighing heavily in the corner office. I couldn't *not* have that copy or we would have a blank page in the newspaper. I went there again. I approached his office a second time. He screamed at me *"fuck right off"*. This happened six or seven times.

I had to process this somehow to get it done. I didn't try to figure out whether he was being mean telling me to fuck off, or because I was young or whatever. That didn't really matter. I just needed to get it done. It wasn't personal. I needed to always remember that.

I couldn't imagine the idea of not solving the issues, saying I couldn't get this out of this creative and asking if he (Dave) would have a word with the creative, then having him say to me, *"Are you not strong enough to do your job?"*

So therefore, I just kept going.

By the seventh time, the creative said, *"I'll do it."* I stood behind him while he typed up the copy. I said nothing. I was very gracious. And then I stamped the copy. Dave got to sign it off by the time it needed to be done. He walked out of the office and went to his meeting. The client approved it, it went into the studio, and then it was out the door ready to go to press.

This type of thing happened every day. Often many times.

It was quite a time and at such a young age a baptism by fire. The key to me was knowing my own strengths. I realized I had a talent to compartmentalize things. I was able to keep many projects in my mind at once. Here I was 21, running traffic at a top London agency. At that time one of the most creative agencies on Earth.

I got myself in a position where I had just enough information on hand to spin many plates. I found I could sift out the information that didn't mean anything. I retained enough information in my brain to single out what mattered. In turn that gave me the ability to connect what needed to be done and therefore connect the dots.

I discovered and then built for myself the reputation of fixing stuff. From there, I grew the wider ability to find others like me - other fixers. As a gang collaboratively, we were able to get any amount of stuff done.

As someone really smart once said, *"If you want something done, ask a busy person."* In every company I've worked with since, I've had the good fortune to seek out the other doers and fixers.

I developed a sixth sense for people who represented my tribe and at the same time systematically removed the word *"no"* from my vocabulary.

I increasingly surrounded myself with people who shared both honesty and transparency. I focused on and attracted people who got all this. I would collaborate and work only with people who wanted the same thing. The right result at the right time.

Throughout it all I sharpened up on that quality that allowed me to pre-empt problems and give us enough time to find better and better results. I became very solution driven.

Traffic meant everything to me because it meant doing everything and that meant really doing it.

I'm 23. I'd had a remarkable time. I didn't realize how much I had had to learn in such a short time. I only came to appreciate just how much far later. You will see in the next few chapters.

I had a growing appreciation and respect for the people I worked with. They had taught me how fearless and brave they were. I learned the importance of developing the right kind of culture. Stuff was always out in the open no one got to hide behind meetings. Nobody dared say they were going to do something for me and not do it.

Dave Trott was the most unbelievable leader, and I was so lucky to have been that close and learnt through watching what he did. He rewarded his staff well when they did the right work, and that meant working hard at the right things. He was always firm but fair, honest, transparent, and open-minded to new ways of doing things. He was a total gentleman, holding doors open for you and extremely family oriented. During those early years, I got to know his family, especially his wife Cathy. Dave always gave you complete backing, and there was an excellent example that will remain with me forever.

The chairman at the time was Mike Greenlees. It was a high pressure moment, so the following story has to be seen in that context. We were pitching for Fosters Lager. Mike Greenlees was practicing for his big moment the following day.

It was around midnight. A lot of people are involved in preparation, and we were all working literally at fever pitch running tight to the challenge. There were 12 scripts required for the pitch the following day.

I remember it vividly. Eventually the scripts had been typed up, stamped, and signed. I went down to the boardroom to hand them over to Mike. In a throw away way he said to me, in front of everyone, *"just leave them there,"* like I was some piece of rubbish.

I said, *"No."*

This was because I knew they had to get into the document. I couldn't stay much longer. Dave had signed them, so he could sign them. This was important, and it was an agreed part of making sure stuff got done. He had an attitude that just made me react. He said again, *"just leave them on the side,"* and again I said, *"No."*

It was quite a moment.

He barged past me and everyone else in the room. He stormed up to see Dave. He said, *"who the hell does she think she is?"* It was the classic, *"doesn't she know who I am?"* I had followed him, and by the time I got to Dave's office I just heard him say, *"Mike, she's just doing her job and you need to appreciate that."*

Dave just knew what was right and never wavered, no matter who it was. He always gave us his total backing if you were doing what was right. He didn't care whether you were the post boy or the Chairman.

I will always cherish his remarks about this episode in an article he wrote a while later:

"Another girl who wouldn't stay a secretary was Nicole Yershon. She developed and ran the first real Traffic system anyone had. What everyone calls Traffic nowadays started there. Nicole was north London, and unstoppable. She wouldn't even let Mike Greenlees, who owned the agency, take the ads if they hadn't been signed off.

We had a department full of stroppy northerners. They wouldn't do anything anyone told them, except Nic. It was like watching that TV program about how sheep dogs herd sheep. For the first time anywhere, the entire agency workload was run by Traffic. Not just the creative department.

Everyone was part of the traffic-system: account men, planners, creatives, right through to production. Every timing plan, every briefing, every debrief, every piece of work on every client was reviewed on time, every week. Small problems were highlighted and solved before they became big problems.

A lot of people confuse inefficiency with creativity. It isn't. It just looks like creativity. Real creativity is taking all the organizational problems away so that people don't have to think about anything but having great ideas."

He taught me many things, but when it came down to the wire, in real life and in business, there were no different personas; it was just one thing, be a good, kind, decent person. He taught me to do my job with an honesty and a purpose that I could live and die by.

There was no other agenda. Simple.

All good things come to an end and a final lesson for me was one of sheer integrity. By now GGT was highly successful but owned by different shareholders.

The management moved to a more financial and profit-driven mentality. Dave was beginning to be seen as difficult. He would never compromise his values around creativity.

This is true not just in the ad industry but in every industry. The economic drivers all too often take precedence over the creative and the pursuit of value.

Dave was ousted from his own company.

But Dave wasn't to be beaten. As you can imagine, he went on to greater and greater things.

He is a prolific author of three books, *Predatory Thinking, Creative Mischief and One Plus One Equals Three*. He's still a big part of my life today.

Problem: How to get things done?

Solution: Fearlessness, tenacity, a self-assured confidence about knowing what needs to be done.

2
STARTUP MENTALITY

*C*hange was always in the air but especially so for me. It was an era of new beginnings. It was also a question of knowing when to move on from GGT. While the solution was to leave, I discovered the problem. I wasn't learning. The curiosity and the challenge had started to wane.

For those of you unfamiliar with it, I should also explain how agencies work. A large global advertising agency is a simple idea on top of a massive machine. The agency (ideally) needs large global clients who (typically) need a single minded *"creative"* campaign placed in all its markets. The agency needs to do this without undue overhead and at maximum profitability. To get the assignment in the first place they need to look the part and then they need to recover the enormous costs that go alongside. Buildings and armies of people who run about a fair bit.

I joined Simons Palmer. It was a startup, with three of the founding members from Gold Greenlees Trott. I knew them and trusted their work ethic and reputations. They were hungry for success and they were doing highly creative and exciting work.

In those days, there was a steady stream of highly glamorous and trendy boutique style agencies. They were quickly famous. It was a new and thrilling time for the ad industry. It was an era where greed was good.

Simons Palmer came out of GGT. We had incredible clients such as, Wrangler, Nike, Sony, and BT. In those days, these clients seemed attracted by the fresh and creative agencies that had blossomed at that time. Together they wanted to push the boundaries of creativity.

It's incredible to look back on it now. It was quite a cohort - a regular ad industry hall of fame. Three of the founding partners were from GGT. Carl Johnson who now founded Anomaly in New York. Simon Clemmow from Clemmow, Hornby Inge (part of WPP). Mark Denton from Coy Communications, Chris Palmer from Gorgeous Films and Paul Simons. The same Paul Simons who ended up being chairman at Ogilvy and who was to employ me much later on.

It was a start up in every sense. Very much a new chapter for me. And back to the drawing board for everyone. We were so small when I joined that I remember my Dad regularly checking them out. He took close looks at their accounts to make sure they were able to look after me and not go out of business.

This start up culture was a revelation to me. I realized very quickly that I loved.

There were 15 people when I first joined. Five of them were founding partners. The difference showed up everywhere. I loved this new role. It was all attitude. A place where you rolled your sleeves up and got shit done. No remote shareholders to please. No more procurement nightmares, nightmares that were stifling creativity in the latter days of GGT.

This was a time when people would research anything that moved. It was possible for a 30-second TV ad to take up to 18 months to get out of the door. Simon's Palmer was brilliant. It was an agile and highly focused team of ex GGT people and Bartle Bogle Hegarty creatives with an unbelievable attitude of pushing the boundaries and making things happen.

The media was handled differently too. Enter a new style of media agency which included Colin Gottlieb and Nick Manning's Manning Gottlieb Media. Colin now runs OMD globally. With media integrated in this way it was both a healthy and hungry way to work. It was a truly capable business. The major learning was that in a start up, you do everything.

If I thought I had fully learned my trade at GGT, I was completely wrong. It was nothing compared to working in a start up. In this world, you quickly learn to do everything or you have a blank page in a newspaper, publication or a blank TV ad spot, it just wouldn't happen. Everyone works together as required to make it work. Most of all, you understood the way a business works. Every single part of the business from every angle, all departments and all platforms.

Stuff really got done. We felt we could change the world. In some ways, we kind of did.

"It felt like being in a small tight-knit family. It was a condensed GGT. It had the spark, creativity, flair, integrity and joie de Vivre of a big agency, but not the intimidation."
- Jo Hollis (Great Friend and Colleague)

What's In A Startup?

One day I remember having a conversation with new entrants to the company. We were talking about new businesses, the *"startup"* and the idea of entrepreneurship. Everyone was deeply involved, and the discussion was deep and engaging.

One particular girl was very intrigued by the conversation but later laughingly confided that she hadn't known what a *"startup"* actually was. Throughout the conversation, the concept hadn't been explained.

It reminded me how easy it is to assume everyone knows the lingo, and how risky that can be.

So, in case you are also unclear - a startup is a bona-fide business but right at its early stage. It's most likely just a few highly dedicated and motivated people with a dream. A few Rough Diamonds if you will. Rough Diamonds believe they've seen a problem and think they have found a solution. They *think*.

They've either left another company or are so driven they've just started, regardless of circumstances. Rough Diamonds and those who run startups, are determined not to be told what to do and insist on being in control of their own destiny to the greatest degree possible.

There I was in just such a startup. I felt like it was my own business. It wasn't especially innovative or entrepreneurial as an industry, it was simply another agency after all. Just the same as countless others unless we made it different. I was always looking around at what was going on outside our company to learn from and integrate what others were doing. Basically, making sure we were doing everything possible to stay ahead of the game and learning from the world.

Countless companies were just popping up everywhere. Wherever I looked there were people doing interesting things.

Everyone I found and investigated led to two or three more. People always asked me how I even knew about some of this stuff, to me I saw it everywhere.

I found out much later that I wasn't looking in the same places everyone else was looking. I was always out of my comfort zone, and that felt comfortable for me.

The startups I found would probably only have one or two people in them. In those days that meant it would be really difficult for a large company to work with them.

All the usual deeply stupid reasons would apply. Procurement policy and doctrine associated with the outdated no-risk culture, too small, not proven, here today/gone tomorrow and no reputation. If you could get their invention into the system then you had the deeply unpleasant and cynical practice of dealing with corporates. Getting start up founders paid took ages and caused cash flow issues.

I knew that these companies were the ones for the future. They were the ones experimenting at the edge, learning how to improve the world we were quite happy to stay safe in. I wasn't so naive that I felt every half-baked idea would be a winner but in a creative industry I knew we needed these new conversations and ideas to stimulate us and keep us on our toes.

I knew it was only possibility - only opportunity and only there for those brave enough to give it a go. All the exciting stuff was happening in between the large organizations. If the large companies were not careful, they would fall between the cracks and miss out on innovation.

A real affinity for helping those out to solve a problem developed inside me. We were a startup too and we didn't have the capability to do everything. Technology was challenging everyone. Either how it was challenging us to change or how we could use it to create change. The more I saw the possibilities in these small companies the more I found that they had a least one core element of the company missing.[1] They would be missing a leader who could make the tough decisions or a tech/marketer who could tell the story.

But there was always a vision, likely distilled and driven by a highly creative person.

Riding The First Wave Of Disruption

Disruption at work became par for the course, but there was relative calm at home. I had got engaged and married quite young to my childhood sweetheart who I knew when I was four and started going out with when I was 14 years old. Simons Palmer had an enormous appetite to push creative boundaries. That meant working with influencers from other industries; fashion, architecture and publishing to name a few. The senior creatives worked with any inspiration and with whatever and whoever they could imagine. There was literally no limit to their appetite for coming up with ideas. We did things that simply hadn't been done before, and as a result we were highly awarded. For me it was an incredible privilege to be at another company with the same values as GGT.

I had to make it happen. Two decades ago things were different on the home front. Work-life balance wasn't a term anyone used

---

[1] As you will read later the idea of startup would eventually take me into more of a mentoring role. This would see me start supporting the start-ups with people like Cisco as they created their big awards campaigns or IBM and Smart Camp. Eventually new forms of networks and initiatives emerged. Accelerators/Incubators were popping up - Seed Camp and Trampery. Collider, for example was also very interesting and educative it was an accelerator and incubator in MaDTech - *A phrase that didn't exist in those days but means Marketing & Advertising Technology.*

at the time. I was married to my childhood sweetheart. I had two amazing children (Claudia and Max), and I was the first woman to go back to work after maternity leave. I took a leave of 18 weeks total. I was allowed to go back on a three-day week to run traffic and creative services. In those days, maternity laws were very different.

If you said you were pregnant you were probably never going back. Not me. I was excited and happy for the opportunity to keep my independence and my maiden name. I needed to get back to what I loved doing.

All of this took place around the time that technology was starting to make a big appearance on the marketing scene.

At both GGT and Simons Palmer my focus was around internal workflow and keeping everything moving. There was a critical balance in all this. I needed to take account of the natural excitement around creativity. The ability to come up with new and brilliant ideas but also making sure the operation matched it and lived up to the same quality.

"We were all on a journey together. The leaders worked on the basis that if they made their staff feel driven yet comfortable, they would get the best out of everyone. I was lucky enough to be one of those people, working with the 'suits' and then in TV production. It was my happiest time in advertising."
- Jo Hollis (Great Friend and Colleague)

During this time, life was blissfully simple, I just needed to know photographers, directors, illustrators and printers. I didn't know it at the time, but impending technology and a brave new digital world would revolutionize my existence.

For me the experience was a great lesson taking place at a great time.

It was a startup. I wasn't there for the money or the glory. I just loved the whole freshness of it and the purity of purpose and ambition. It was never really my goal to build an empire, but rather to be part of a great creative team. It was always about doing real things. Things that mattered and needed to get done.

I have never been driven by being on a board and having many people report into me. That then involves you doing a totally other job function which is administration or reviews for staff or reporting structures. I didn't see that as interesting to do for eight hours a day. My driver was autonomy, not groupthink decision making and meetings for meeting's sake.

It was a real balance of course. Too much confidence can be fatal for a startup. Rash decisions made without proper research aren't a good idea - ever. But that is different than taking informed risks and failing. Failure is one of the most important factors when it comes to moving forward. Whoever keeps trying will keep failing as well. That is just the cycle of success. The trick is to keep moving forward no matter what. That is what Rough Diamonds do!

Failures line the road towards achieving any big success and failures are how you know what *doesn't work*, so you can be confident when you find what *does*. It's how I learnt then and how I learn now. Failing, learning, moving forward and laying the foundation for evolving through any innovation cycle. Whatever the problem, the solution can generally be found through experimentation by bold and creative individuals.

Digital would come to transform me completely. It would tear me out from that uncomplicated internal perspective into an immense and vibrant external one. I would have to learn to look out into the marketplace and understand, connect and partner with those driving digital forward.

It was an exciting new era and one that was just beginning to emerge.

My role within traffic and creative services was starting to come to an end. I had built a solid reputation of being a fixer. The Chairman Paul Simons had just negotiated to sell the agency. It merged with

TBWA (another agency), then it was merged with GGT and then BST (another agency). GGT was the company I came from. I'd come full circle. The final owners would be Omnicom.

And then, as Simons Palmer merged with TBWA they needed to move to Whitfield Street. Paul asked me if I would be part of the team to help move them. He trusted that I would be able to do it. I'd obviously never done anything like that before. This was a sign for me to move away from doing traffic to be the person who people would ask to fix things.

I ended up moving the joint agency (that was to become an agency of four) into the new building. This was a major moment in my life - big agency culture hit me. It was classic, the right-hand didn't know what the left and was doing.

There were silos - four companies merging into one. Everything was a reinvention of the wheel. Every day another drama. People were there one minute and gone the next. It was as if they had gone through some trapdoor never to be seen again. It was definitely not an environment that I enjoyed working in but one that afforded me valuable life lessons.

I didn't know it at the time but learning to navigate the big agency dynamic would prove to be a vital foundation for when I started working at Ogilvy, one of the biggest ad agencies in the world.

"Simons Palmer was a heady mix of contradictions, insecurities, egos and enormous self-belief. I remember the phrase 'Pearls before swine' being used as a way of psyching the team before a client meeting. The senior team were impressive. Razor sharp and compelling. We did some great work. Legacy work. Crosstown Traffic on Wrangler. 'Can you kick it on Nike' and all the award-winning posters."
- Karina Parker (Great Friend and Colleague)

Hardening The Diamond

It struck me around this time that perhaps I wasn't the same as other people. I always loved the saying *"I'm humble enough to know I'm no better than anyone else, yet wise enough to know I'm different."*

I know that sounds a bit strange, but I wasn't as uncomfortable as everyone else with all the changes all the time. People talked about change as a bad thing and something to be battled with - to defend the status quo at all costs. Change was a bad thing. I was always the odd one out. I loved it. To me, change always brings new ideas and provides a chance to create new opportunities.

At the same time, I noticed my views were forming. I had an opinion about things. I've always believed that conversation was at the root of progress, but I've always thought conversations are better when people have strong or well-constructed opinions. Opinions of their own. No right or wrong, just a difference of opinion. It wasn't for me to judge but rather embrace how everyone felt and try and come up with solutions to fix problems.

I have never held the view that I am always right. In those days, it was useful if I put something out there just to get people to come back at me with their own view. Otherwise stuff just happened without discussion. It was more likely projects would go haywire. I couldn't afford for things to go off the rails. If they did, I would go off with them.

I've made a list of the things that I knew at this point in my career. These are the things principles I would live and die by:

The 8 Principles Of A Rough Diamond - My Mantra For Survival

1. **Develop Curiosity** - Learn to notice what others don't. Things that I knew would be important just didn't seem so to others. But curiosity uncovers hidden opportunities.
2. **Learn How To Learn** - Improvement and innovation can be as easy as trying something and observing the result, taking

that into account and trying something else. Think of this as learning by doing.

3. **Know How To Say What Matters** - My mentor Dave Trott taught me the meaning of straight talk. By speaking the truth, we go places far faster. There may be short term pain, but the long-term results are always worth it.

4. **It Pays To Be Honest** - When you don't speak the truth, problems quickly find their way to your door. Sugarcoating doesn't work because it allows issues to go unchecked. That's just stupid in a fast-moving creative environment.

5. **Become a Rapid Processor** - How quickly can you see and respond to what matters? Trust and act on your intuition, as it is formed from experience and allows you to process and respond to input and stimulus fast. When others are debating an issue, start the process of simply fixing it.

6. **Always Open** - Life doesn't wait. Things need to get done. Understand that the reward is one of achievement. Your achievements mean the team achieves. The team achieving means we all achieved.

7. **Being Clear** – Be honest and have something to show for your work so there is no doubt in people's minds. Speak plainly. Like Dave would always say, *"simple is smart, complicated is stupid. Doubt is the enemy. Clarity kills doubt."*

8. **No Off Switch** - People need to understand that you won't stop at no. No is fine when we are going the wrong way. No is not OK when someone is delaying the endeavor of the team. Learn not to stop at no. Tenacity and persistence help turn NO into YES.

Developing Mentality

"I have nothing to offer but blood tears toil and sweat."
- Winston Churchill

I had started to identify the characteristics for what made me. That which informed my opinions and drove me to evolve in the way that I did. These principles were becoming my guiding force, developing my mentality.

Mentality is a very interesting thing. Again, it was early on my journey and I was just beginning to understand the idea of why mentality is so important.

The required mentality of a startup only became apparent to me later on. I didn't consciously sit down and create it. I couldn't have- it formed all in its own through the battering ram of experience. Every day a blistering reality of seeing what did or didn't work.

Looking back, I can describe my mentality in one word: **fearless.** Each day started with a challenge ringing in my ears. Whatever that challenge was each day, and there would be many, I said, *"I'm going to sort it out."* Once that was spoken out loud in my head it was fixed.

Every problem I encountered, every single obstacle I just had to move out of the way. And as a result, I eventually arrived at an initial set of ideas that underpinned my *"Fearless Manifesto".*

The Fearless Manifesto

- **It's Important To Ignite The Tribe** - I saw that a few good people could rip up trees. Even a forest. Sometimes we had to do that and then build a mountain in its place. The only way I could do that was by igniting the same desire in others. I tapped into their passion and made them willing partners in the challenge.
- **Developing Nerve** - the critics would wail. I felt the heat of the critics. Those that didn't get it and were never going to. People who just saw change as a threat. There are many of those out there. I didn't care. My obsession was the achievement not the compromise. Achieving is not a popularity contest. Creativity isn't easy. Mediocrity is hard.

- **Create Simplicity** - Boiling things down to their essence has to happen in real time. I didn't have the luxury of time. Time is often the enemy. If I couldn't get my point across simply there was going to be a problem. It would mean repeat cycles, wasted work, frustrated people. Complexity is not a viable option.
- **The Dawning Of An Alchemist** - These years taught me sleight of hand, industrial magic. I had to make stuff out of nothing. Things that were readily at hand can be repurposed to do different things on different days. We can all set our hands to many purposes. There is no place for ego or grandiose titles.
- **Take A Breath** - There is nothing to be gained from adding to any tension, other than more tension that is. I learnt to stare into the whirlwind of pressure and anxiety because that's an ever-present part of any creative process. I managed to stay removed from the fray. Never adding to the emotion. Never sweating the small stuff.
- **Work Life Balance** - I found out that I have a passion and a vocation for doing things. Not talking about doing things or maybe imagining doing things but *actually* doing things. I never had a problem with balance. Rather, I loved my work and that *was* my life. These two things can feed each other. I feel very lucky that I found my true vocation early on as it simplified my purpose and still drives me to this day. Whatever the task, I make things happen!

"It was my first job in advertising. Rather intimidating but exciting. We were on the up and getting talked about. We were described as a 'Hot Shop' and it felt like we had a golden touch."
- Karina Parker (Great Friend and Colleague)

Problem: When do you know when to move on?

Solution: When you are not learning, and the curiosity starts to wane.

3
THE IRRESISTIBLE FORCE AGAINST IMMOVABLE OBJECTS

I Left Simons Palmer

7he big collision of TBWA, GGT and BST was all a little too much. The overlapping roles and having made the move mentally I was *"job done."* I'm not one to invent a role where one doesn't exist, and I was thinking (I was only thinking) – that it was time to move, and guess what…

The phone call from Dave Trott couldn't have been more serendipitous. Actually, I had found my whole life full of serendipity just by saying the word *yes*!

Dave had set himself up with another agency. His third with his name above the door.

The agency was called Walsh-Trott-Chick-Smith (WTCS). As well as being unemployable, like many a great entrepreneur, Dave had created another place from which to launch great creative work. You can't keep a good man down.

He needed help with his new agency. And partly because I was now a mum, he took me on a three-day week. I will remember his words forever - *"Nic, your three days are better than most people's five."*

It was a period of changing attitudes towards new mums working part time. Prior to this it was frowned upon, or at least something you wouldn't shout about. Society seemed to have its own plans laid out for people. I wasn't that bothered about what society wanted for me. Especially if that meant compromising.

Technology was starting to allow people to work from anywhere, and for the next 18 months I was back - doing *both* the traffic and creative services role.

It allowed me to put everything I had learnt at GGT & Simons Palmer (with creative services & traffic skills) to the test again.

In many ways, I could come back afresh to the principles and lessons learnt. The difference was I could merge the creative services part of the role with the overall traffic; the *get stuff done* part. I could show even more efficiency and effectiveness and, in my mind,, be even more innovative. I had seen a bunch of new ideas and technologies that I could bring to bear. This was going to be a new era of learning and pushing the boundaries.

For me it was another even more privileged period learning how to deliver effectiveness efficiently.

I knew I had an incredibly easy boss and mentor in Dave. I understood his simple ethic and his focused discipline. He was always firm but fair and there was never any ambiguity with his needs or wants. It was all very simple and straightforward.

What appealed to me was the absence of micromanagement. Something that was starting to happen in the previous role and especially as the four companies moved closer together.

It occurred to me that the bigger a company got, the more ridiculous and totally irrelevant their processes became. The more that happened, the more the right hand completely ignored what the left hand was doing. Ironies popped up everywhere in those situations. When it came to communication at the communications agency - it was a rare spot.

I now found myself again, inside yet another highly charged creative environment. It was running like a Swiss watch.

Around 18 months into it all, I received a call from Paul Simons, the chairman at Simons Palmer and Managing Director at GGT. It was January 2000. He was now the CEO of Ogilvy & Mather, the main advertising agency in London. This was big. One of the world's best known and certainly largest agencies.

Paul Simon and Jeff Quilter had a chat with me about the opportunity to bring Ogilvy into the 21st century. I thought about it for a split second.

What a great prospect! I was in.

Ogilvy was based in Canary Wharf in East London. The location was great as I lived in the East. A much easier drive in each day, and still a three-day week, and I could still be a mum.

Everything up until this point would be vital for me in this new role. All the capabilities would need to be brought to a head to do what was needed - and at a global scale. The big excitement for me was not knowing exactly what was needed but having a mandate to find it and get it done.

This was a massive part of what drove me. That was the ideal challenge for me. Put it like that and I'm all over it. I would be able to figure it out.

No one knew what was needed in those days. Both life and business were starting to get seriously interesting. There was this big thing – DIGITAL! Many of us knew it was coming, and that it was going to be exciting. Many didn't believe it was coming. They would get crushed.

Paul and Jeff didn't know how it should look, but they knew it was needed. They didn't even do a proper job description (HR would have been appalled). They just trusted me.

I can't state clearly enough how important it is to have senior level buy-in to innovate within a large organization. They had the trust, the transparency, the courage and the commitment to allow me - an intrapreneur - to flourish.

They knew I had what it took. They knew going digital would involve collaborations and partnerships in this new dawning era. They knew I would go at it with a steely determination, tenacity and *"make it happen"* attitude. Dragging the agency kicking and screaming into the new century.

I look back now and realize I had never actually created a CV (curriculum vitae). My reputation has always preceded me. I've always been a bit of a maverick and certainly an anomaly. That kind of definition defies most traditional job roles. We were all happy. They had no idea what the solutions were. I was in my element identifying the challenge at hand, clarifying each part of the problem, and finding the right solution.

"Bloody Paper Everywhere…"

Paul Simons had uncovered some inconvenient realities. He said working in the agency in those times was like working in the civil service. There was *"bloody paper everywhere"* It wasn't just at Ogilvy, but being so large meant that was one hell of a lot of paper! Most of it entirely useless and never reviewed.

To get anything done needed a job number. To get a job number you needed to go to the finance lady. The finance lady wrote the number down. She wrote the number down many times.

In fact, she wrote the same number on many bits of paper. Someone would eventually get a pink bit, a yellow bit, a blue bit, and who-knows-what-color bit. You went away with your particular colored bit of paper while the lady wrote it down in *"the book."*

If she was at lunch, and the book was locked in the drawer, and you'd lost your yellow bit of paper, and you needed to order a runner, then you were dead. Game over.

If that wasn't enough paper for you, every week the creative secretaries did a roundup of what everyone was working on. On paper.

Given all the various colors, numbers, handwritten instructions and labels it was a small miracle anyone knew anything. In fact, that's exactly what happened. Nobody knew anything. But at least there was plenty of paper to prove it.

Each week, hearts would sink as you would be presented with a really thick wad of paper that told you nothing and couldn't really be trusted.

You couldn't see who was busy or who wasn't. You couldn't tell who was on a shoot, or who was on holiday, and when you piled up all the paper, you couldn't even see who was in the room.

All the great things that I had seen and done over the previous decade or so with GGT & Simons Palmer weren't even on their radar.

How did this ever work? **Spoiler Alert: It didn't**.

So, I created what I had created at GGT & Simons Palmer - a workflow. A procedure that could be read on one piece of paper, actually it was one page of a spreadsheet. The workflow system was digital.

In Case You Were Wondering How It Worked

I mean it's not that hard!

You had a creative team written in at the top (art director & copywriter), then across the top, you had a row that said what was in the creative department - within concept development.

The next row across, would be what was with the client awaiting approval or in research. The third row would show what was in production.

Then at the bottom it would tell you instantly if anyone was away on holiday or on shoots.

That was it.

Just one bit of paper that showed (at least) ten teams across the top and all of the agency workload what was going on at a glance.

This was what was needing to be digitized. So that a job number opened would then raise a creative brief.

The brief would drop in. Firstly, into the creative team's row, and then move seamlessly down the rows, until it disappeared. That meant it was either on air or in the press or on poster sites.

This led to a few redundancies. You could really see who was busy, and who wasn't, what everyone was working on, and what they weren't - and where they were in the workflow (or weren't).

Digital meant there was no hiding place. It was the first sign of time and cost efficiency savings - not pleasant for many who had been able to hide. It was the start of things to come. There was no turning back from technology. Most importantly, you couldn't stop it. You either had to embrace it, change with it and keep moving forward or you're going backwards, even if you're standing still.

This was a perfect challenge but at a bigger scale than anything I'd ever done before. It was vital to know but really difficult to get your head around understanding how it should work. We needed to know what we were capable of and better understand the workload and resources that we had.

We had no way of knowing how to manage and improve the performance of the teams - here we were in such a large agency. And they wanted to go digital!

Because no one really knew what anyone was doing, the first thing I did was to focus and prioritize. I chose to move three areas from analog to digital. They would provide the foundations for what was to come later.

The first one we digitized was a workflow system. So, we were able to all see digitally exactly what everyone was working on.

We needed a real team to pull this all off.

We used a great little company and system called RPS. We didn't need an army of managers, fancy methods or crazy overhead. We just needed good people. We were lucky. In RPS there were a few amazing people. They just listened carefully to what we needed doing, took the strain and made it happen.

The workflow system was to be attached to the current Ogilvy & Mather finance system. In this case, the supplier was DDS Systems. They were already being used within WPP Group PLC., the holding company, and across all their agencies.

The third thing to be digitized and created was a digital asset management system. We were at the start of the digital transformation. It was true change within the entire organization. We never thought it was going to be an easy journey because no one is ever keen on change.

Little did we know.

Although, I didn't call it by these names 17 years ago, we would need a lot of luck, wizardry and alchemy to pull this off. Change is never easy but changing something that has been in place for 30 or 40 years is beyond hard.

The Following Will Give You A Glimpse Into My Mad Men Challenge

In an agency, managing assets is a core process. We wanted to make that automated and make it easy to retrieve or deploy these assets, ideally in seconds. For that we needed what is now known as a digital asset management system (DAMS). (If you say those words slowly, they really do make sense). We realized we needed one. Except there was one problem. They didn't exist

We had to go and make one and as fast as we could. We had some serious work to do. There were these big master tapes affectionately known as U-Matics. Ogilvy had 10,000 of them going back to the 50's. They were held in expensive storage buildings in South London.

I made the case to the Finance Director that the storage cost was greater than simply rolling up our sleeves and getting it done.

Sleeves Rolled Up And Doing It Meant Working Closely With Great People

We used TAG & Steve Parrish, (an industry pioneer who later sold out and moved to become Chairman of Crystal Palace Football Club) to implement the first DAM system. I helped them develop the workflow and then worked with the programmers to build the DAMS.

There was also an amazing man called Mick. There's almost always someone called Mick. He saved and scanned hundreds of thousands of mechanicals & transparencies. If you've never seen what's involved in saving and scanning even one of these things, then just imagine a mountain of pain and jump off.

We did one version of every printed ad we had ever done, and the rest was thrown into the world's biggest ever collection of skips. When it came to digitizing every single tape, there was another wonderful man called Keith Aveling. Like your favorite teacher, you always remember people like these. In East London, we have a saying, *"Salt of the Earth"* - that's what these men were.

Keith was the essence of helpful. He had been at Ogilvy forever - at least 40 years. His knowledge inspired me. He had worked alongside so many great people. To this incredible list, I would add my good friend Natalie Sutton. She ran the edit facility at Ogilvy. It was called Diva.

They all helped me. And along with a few Ravensbourne College students interning from Greenwich London (where everyone thinks time comes from), we cut a very long story as short as humanly possible. It was an enormous undertaking. At the end of this work, I purchased them the latest Apple product at the time - a brand new iPod - as a sign of appreciation.

In a successful enterprise, there's always a team behind you. This was 17 years ago. Today people still talk about digitizing all their assets but never actually do it. It was a massive achievement and one none of us will forget.

That Finance Thing

There was a constant issue with write off's and the money involved that we would never get back. It's a perennial issue in ad agencies. This is where job bags just can't be reconciled. Our initiative was to merge the RPS workflow system with the DDS finance system.

As a result, nothing could get put in hand with a supplier before a client had signed off on the estimate. Not surprisingly, this was the hardest initiative of all.

Now think about this little classic.

I found all this out after the system had been implemented. One day I heard something vaguely familiar whirring away in the corner of a room. I approach this thing. Sure enough, the sound of a printer. It was doing its thing, printing away.

People were still printing off purchase orders to commission work the old way, not getting approvals by going through the agreed system.

The old DDS printer was still in the corner of the office. So, one night, when everyone had gone home, I threw it away. It took them four days to pluck up the courage to ask where it had gone. Someone finally asked, *"what has happened to the DDS order printer?"* I replied, *"Oh, I gave it a Viking's burial, as we don't use that system anymore."*

A very loud silence ensued.

From here on, we were on the *"new digital process highway"* of working or the *"no way"* of working. Easy? No. Necessary? Yes!

To pull all this off, I worked closely with IT to implement and integrate the digital systems & trained around 300 people in the building - across all departments.

Two fabulously supportive IT individuals, Jamie McClellen (who is now JWT Worldwide CTO) and Andrew Cowan, and all of the Ogilvy IT team. These unsung heroes of large organizations get taken for granted. I never took them for granted. They were crucial in helping me implement these changes.

I found, with the implementation of new digital systems and ways of working, there would be around a 12 week pain period, about the same as with a baby sleeping through the night. Once you cut off all old ways of doing things, and enough time passes, people generally can't remember how it used to be done.

It was important for them to trust the new system. It's like when you get an alert on your smartphone. The system is calling for an update, and you put it off for as long as possible. You're scared you may lose contacts, texts or your images. Then you go through the pain of the upgrade and the user interface is all new. It's a pain. For a short while you can't get to things as quickly. Then, you see it's all much better.

This is exactly the pain that people experience - but after a while, they forget. We realized that we always needed to help guide people through and ride that pain barrier.

A real insight for me at this time, which is now the norm, was to stand in the shoes of users and not be the least bit fazed by the shiny technology. Our wonderful IT directors, Jamie McClellen & Andrew Cowan would call me the *"thick user,"* meaning if I could use it, then they knew everyone could use it. Nobody wanted to be left with a rampaging white elephant of a system that no one would ever use.

They were two fabulously supportive and extremely smart IT individuals. Indeed, all of the Ogilvy IT team were the unsung heroes of the organization. People often take the IT department for granted. I never did. They were crucial in helping implement these changes and digitize the agency.

This was the start of understanding change. It wasn't for the faint hearted. It was a time of incredible learnings, working with people outside the agency, people who were doing interesting amazing things and people who thought like me.

I knew they were the future. But I also knew that none of this would have worked without the backing of senior management. Without their support and mandate, change would have never happened.

Changing human behavior is at the root of all this. And changing people's behavior is bloody hard. My entire challenge began and ended with getting the right people on my side. I soon found out there were some people you would be able to connect with immediately and they would understand and embrace it. There would be others who just wouldn't. I had to develop ways of dealing with both.

Problem: How do you move a company from an analog to a digital world?

Solution: It's all about the people, not necessarily the technology. Get people comfortable with doing things that are uncomfortable.

4

THERE IS NO NO

Things had started to happen. I was making waves. Waves weren't happy and they were inevitably pushing back. That's a great sign that change is having an effect.

I saw something else about change recently. It took a snapshot from around 100 years ago. Our grandparents were bouncing around. It reminded me that as we look forward it's hard to imagine how different things can get and yet looking back, just how much change actually happens. If only we could make it easier for our colleagues to be more comfortable with it. Imagine how much more we could achieve.

In 1915, the average life expectancy for men was 47 years. Fuel for cars was sold in chemists only. Only 14% of our homes had a bath. Only 8% of the homes had a telephone. The maximum speed limit in most cities was 10 mph. The tallest structure in the world was the Eiffel Tower.

Whether this is to be believed or not, shepherding in change successfully is about making the uncomfortable as comfortable as possible. But that will only work after there's been a period of time. Time for natural acceptance.

It's actually strange given the topic and the length of time it takes sometimes but patience isn't really a strength of mine. Yet, that is what it takes to see change take effect in some areas of life.

Needless to say, I've had to learn more and more patience over the years. As the centuries roll on the rate of change has increased but you wouldn't think so in some of the big organizations I've seen. This was a large institution and implementation of any solution would only work by spotting those small and subtle opportunities to get myself in. I became a bit of a marine on special operations. I got to a result by being highly tactical, using stealth and by getting a few key influencers on my side. This would never work as a Big Bang.

I knew my mission. To dismantle the analog world and start to build a digital one. Under the cover of night and camouflage face paint I turned my attention to the edit facility (this is called post production, it is where editing happens usually on TV commercials or anything that involves a moving image). At Ogilvy, as I mentioned earlier, it was called Diva.

I had a strong feeling that content was going to become a big deal. So, I thought that would be a perfect place to make some valuable and high impact changes.

A revolution was in the air and it was called total disruption. Business really wakes up and pays attention if something happens to attack their business model. Disruption in the advertising industry is all about attacking the business model, as you will read later.

If you run an ad agency and you make your money by getting people to watch ads, this was deeply significant. Our beloved 30-second TV ads were going to be skipped. Strange new services were popping up like moles across a finely manicured lawn. With names like TiVo, Sky+, and Virgin all starting to make an appearance. Remember this was happening around 15 years ago.

To survive and grow, disruptors need the support of the very incumbents whose industry they seek to revolutionize.

In this way, TiVo was a prime example of a disruptive innovation a game changing technology, product, or business model. At this time, it was mainly used in the USA, not so much in Europe. But the revolution was bubbling away. It was happening. We felt it.

A disruptive innovation is financially unviable and truly hard for incumbents, but it can provide a valuable foothold for new entrants the few new entrants, that is, who survive these David vs. Goliath showdowns. A fight that's often to the death and which typically pit startups with few resources against well-established brands.

When TiVo burst on the scene in 1999, its digital video recorder (DVR) set in motion a profound transformation of the TV industry and the public's viewing habits.

This ended the long standing practice of broadcast networks dictating when people had to watch programs and how much companies had to pay to advertise during certain precious time slots.

Disruptors face a fundamental paradox; to survive and grow, they need the support of the very incumbents whose industry they seek to revolutionize. After all, a TiVo box wouldn't have been much good without a compatible TV or cable system to hook up to. But established firms have every reason to resist or even retaliate against an upstart firm that threatens their way of doing business.

For a regular fee to these services, people could simply avoid the ads. In those days, not everyone in the country knew this was happening. In the UK, it was mainly restricted to the London area at first, but I could see something was definitely in the air. It needed dealing with.

To me this was a business issue. It was about pounds, dollars and revenue and how we could stay ahead of inevitable challenges to our bottom line. I looked at new ways of doing things to achieve cost and time efficiency savings.

It seemed obvious to me that we could make money from the edit facility. With the blessing from the Head of Broadcast at the time, I relaunched it as a new business called Domain with 12 members of staff and a fully-fledged post production facility.

I employed someone who came in from the Mill (another edit facility who won an Oscar for their post-production work on the film Gladiator) and continued to partner with them with a branch of the Mill in the main agency. This came complete with a *"flame"* suite; all of this was now available for our express use inside the main agency.

The Domain team were amazing individuals, ready to try anything new that had never been tried before. I will always be in awe of their can-do attitude - so I give thanks to them all here.

This partnership gave us much needed experience in monetizing the results of all the work. We could at last justifiably charge as a profit not a cost center. This was the opposite of the high cost implementations of digital software systems which had preceded this wave of digitization.

Next, we removed all of the expensive Avid editing software and installed Apple's Final Cut Pro. This was in the very early years of Apple implementing their global vision for seamless, low-cost, high quality digital delivery. This was also the dawning of the era of kids editing high production value films on their laptops and smart devices on the London Underground on the way to work.

I was in my element. Although many of those affected by this change looked at me with some trepidation, I knew this was the right path.

By now my children, Claudia and Max, were nine and seven. I wanted to continue my career full time and not just part time. I could see clearly what was going to happen with the industry and technology and I wanted to be part of that. Home was still quite settled; the children were not teenagers yet and it was a good time. I was always fortunate to have the most wonderful nanny, called Cherry, who was with us when Claudia was 4 and Max was 2.

Cherry had a child of her own and it worked well. She was like my close friend and an older sister to the children. We went through two of her pregnancies with her and managed to get by and struggle with her maternity leave. It was because she always felt like a member of our family.

Once all the children were growing, Cherry's three and my two, it was like the Brady Bunch with school runs and meal times.

In the end, I had to deliver the sad news to Cherry, when Claudia was 17, that she wasn't needed anymore as Claudia was able to drive. We all stay in touch regularly. When you have any job, you really do need the backup of great people around you to get by and do what you love. I always have appreciated people like Cherry in mine and my kids' lives. I really felt I needed to get back to my career in earnest again.

I decided to go back to work five days a week. I had an itch that I needed to scratch. There were so many things that I could see we could do. I had hundreds of unanswered questions in my head.

My mind was full of why, why not, when, and what if. I was fueled and intoxicated by possibility. This was the first time I realized I had tapped into this *"entrepreneurial"* spirit inside me. The idea fired me to do even more.

I bought into the digital vision completely. For me it wasn't *if* but *when*. Digital was so obvious to me. It was going to affect our industry comprehensively. It was going to affect every industry and it would do so exponentially.

That meant highly exciting times ahead. It was a digital revolution for sure. There was no turning back, and it thrilled me.

I started to look around and found some like-minded and equally misunderstood people. They were everywhere and sitting quietly waiting to be inspired. They sat amongst some very dispirited others. I couldn't save everyone.

Even today I still meet people who look and sound like they've lived in a cave for the last 20 years. They completely missed the floods. They aren't interested in social media, they don't understand the digital transformation in their industries, and they seem disinterested about the massive changes that are eating their lunches.

I felt something else happen too - outside the business. The network effect started to go into overdrive. I began to build and continue to connect up a merry band of digital refugees. We understood each other, and we spoke the same language; we just didn't know what it was called just yet, but it felt very good.

I was to find that I had an intuition for spotting brave and curious individuals. Having read Seth Godin's blog about Hunters and Farmers, I saw the same. It was the Hunter mentality that would help in pushing forward the boundaries. The future intrapreneur.

There it was. My future was digital disruption. And to me that was indistinguishable from the future of the advertising industry.

I've always felt that advertising, branding, and marketing should embrace all forms of marketing communications. To that we could now add many new avenues, channels that could be viewed on mobile phones. Streaming was now a thing and new ideas and innovations were sprouting up almost daily. It was an incredible time, and it had only just begun.

Each day, the possibilities were mounting, and they became increasingly interesting.

OgilvyOne was the direct marketing division of the Ogilvy Group. It was a big moment when it acquired one of the first famous digital agencies in London, NoHo.

It soon became known as *"Ogilvy Interactive."* This allowed the group to fast forward the reputation for digital direct marketing. NoHo's business model was referred to in those days as one-to-one. That meant creating a unique (one-to-one) relationship with customers. It gave us a much more project based revenue stream.

They were hungry, and their approach was to continuously increase their revenues by adding more and more projects. This was very different to the advertising agency model, which made most of their revenue by big monthly retainers from large global brands.

The differences were enormous. The agency idea was based on *"broadcasting to many"* and making big noise. Traditional advertising of TV and print took a long time to produce and were extremely expensive to implement.

In comparison, the new digital era allowed us to target people with precision at far lower costs and start to tailor the messages and offers in many more interesting ways. This was also the start of the data revolution for us. We didn't really know how big this was to become but that's a whole other chapter.

Disruption now moved from the technology itself to attacking the commercial model at the heart of the industry. This was the start of a massive change to come on the business side of things.

I remember thinking that for me this period was like being let loose in a candy store. I was so excited with all the different things happening, I started to send emails around to all staff. I was naively thinking that they would be as interested as I was.

I wanted them all to know what was happening. I remember so clearly sending out a note saying, *"guys, there is something out there called Facebook. You should really get to grips with it. It's exciting."* I got one email back saying, *"Stop spamming me!"*

It was a great insight. Yet again, it showed me that not everyone had the same curiosity for this stuff as me. However, I wasn't deterred.

I just needed to surround myself with the hunters, continue to be stealthy and be gracious that the farmers were not on the same journey. Disruption would catch them later.

Undeterred, I started an email group with the Ogilvy Interactive guys called *"Lon Labs."*

It was right there that we started sharing all this wonderful stuff. We shared everything that was happening in digital and the across mobile space. We shared stuff on social media, gaming, augmented reality. If it was digital, we knew about it. We teared into it, ripped it apart, understood it, and told whoever signed up to hear about it.

The Lon Lab email group was a closed group. To get in you needed to get your name to IT and register. It started out with just 15 of us and ended up around 1000 globally. My thirst for whatever was new continued; it's never stopped. Meaningful sharing meant conversations got started. Conversations that had never happened before.

The right and the most relevant people got excited - but that didn't mean the day job got diverted. It just made it more bearable I guess for the curious few.

I love this way of working. Exploring the outside world and bringing in exciting knowledge happening outside the agency. Making it valuable for those inside. This was what I had in common with the Ogilvy Interactive team. And I began to see I was gradually moving away from the traditional advertising agency people.

I've always focused on having great relationships with suppliers. And now these lessons started reaping real benefits. One supplier in particular was the digital partner of the Mill. They were the distribution part of the Mill, they were brand new, and they were called BEAM (I give thanks and respect also for the early days of those wonderful visionaries to make this a reality.) In reality, they hadn't done anything yet. They were looking to revolutionize the digital distribution of TV commercials and Moving Image content.

This was a marriage made in heaven. I could see a significant solution to one mega problem at Ogilvy. Getting huge files anywhere was a total pain, and to some extent still is today. Nobody told me it couldn't be done, so I was always trying to push the boundaries of what could be. Certainly no one had tried this before.

At this time, the world was crazy with roadworks. Copper pipes were starting to be laid everywhere to connect up the entire world. In London, every street was dug up every day. You couldn't move without seeing workers in orange jackets with their burrowing equipment. It was so bad people emigrated from London.

This meant we were technically able to distribute all these big file things quickly, easily and effortlessly. It signaled the potential of moving away from tapes and expensive couriers clogging up every reception area around the world.

I decided to do a partnership with the Mill and BEAM. It was that early on in their lives that they hadn't released their own website yet. But we had already built and trialed a complete model for Mattel. Mattel used to do 150 commercials a year that all came out of Los Angeles.

As they finished the commercial, they would make a master tape. They would then send 70 copies of each tape to every country; about 70 global markets. This would involve making a different version which would cost around $600 for both the master and couriers.

Sometimes, for example in the Baltic states, everything would get stuck for a month. This made a nonsense of the timing plan. We would have to allow a month. Imagine the complexity, imagine the cost, imagine the frustration, and imagine me!

It drove me crazy. I was fixated by the need to fix it.

Even on simple math, it just didn't add up. And therefore, rather than doing tapes and couriers everywhere, we would start to do digital distribution of TV commercials. These massive files were stacked up into what was called a Targa sequence. This was the name given for a file size, where you have an enormous TV commercial file, shrunk to a much smaller size to fit it down the copper pipes.

Put simply, this was an upload of the TV commercial in one country and you would be able to download it in another country.

The word and concept of *"upload"* seems normal today, but back then it was the most difficult thing for people to imagine. It was like voodoo.

People stood back a distance from the screens as if expecting a bat to fly out of it and steal their liver.

People were still expecting tapes and couriers. So, they would phone up and say where is my TV commercial. I would say I haven't sent it. They would then scream and shout saying, *"you're going to make me miss my air date."*

I would say, *"go to your post house and download it."* I would then have to explain the concept of download. They often didn't really believe it was real. It was a painful but hugely important time.

At this point, where most people would perhaps give up, I was reminded by a poster that was given to me by my father, that was given to him in his early days in the advertising industry. I had it up on my wall. It was a quote from Machiavelli's The Prince:

"It must be considered that there is nothing more difficult to carry out, nor more doubtful of success, nor more dangerous to handle, than to initiate a new order of things."

For the leaders and the enlightened, the value and performance increase was obvious, but there were always those that remained skeptical. Luckily for me I had incredible buy in from the chairman at the time in Ogilvy London.

He was the most wonderful chap - Mike Walsh, who is still now a trusted friend and mentor and in New York there was Brian Fetherstonhaugh and John Seifert, who is now Ogilvy's global CEO.

If anyone had a major problem, I would say to them go speak to these guys. And so, digital distribution was born.

The partnership with BEAM/The Mill was a major success. I'm still very much in contact years later with Katie and Noreen who still work there. Our access to the *"Flame"* suite meant that they would finish editing in Canary Wharf. We would send it down the line and upload it. It would go directly to the TV stations.

It was simply bigger, better, stronger, and faster. Clients loved it. Procurement loved it. The agency loved it. But no money was really to be made with it. Well not in the old model anyway.

Now we really needed to think differently. It was at this instrumental point that I met Liri Andersson, who was to be one of my closest friends.

Rory Sutherland introduced me to her. He was the vice chairman of OgilvyOne and absolutely understood my value and what I was trying to create.

He respected my intrapreneurial spirit. At the time with BEAM, I had an idea to use the same way to distribute content for TV commercials - to then distribute content in retail stores. Up until now, retail stores had TV screens and played the same content over and over again. The same music.

What if they could play one piece of content to one screen on one floor and another piece of content on another floor.

What if they wanted to get rid of some stock, perhaps they could change the content at different times of the day or to different screens. What if they wanted to do flash discounts on certain items that were not selling well?

This was all possible with the BEAM system. We were chatting to Ford dealerships about this. What if each dealership could show totally different content at different times of the day?

Liri had been working with WPP and retail, as well as Cisco and Mindshare. She was an INSEAD MBA graduate (Business School outside of Paris) and read business books in bed.

I hadn't had a University life. I had gone to a finishing school in Hampstead. My curiosity and thirst for business was there though and together with Liri our thinking was ignited. We were off!

I managed to convince the Ogilvy advertising CEO, Gary Leih, that she was crucial if we intended to get to the more serious business discussions with our clients. To actually be at the boardroom table.

Liri had the expertise to do this. She was employed with the title *"business in creativity and vice versa."*

We spent many days working together as a force for change. Liri created an amazing educational program for account teams to understand the major changes happening in the world around digital and technology, why should our clients care, and how could we make money in alternative ways. This was called *"Eyeops."* We saw that the creative agency was going to come up against the consultants, like Accenture, Bain & Co, McKinsey. Liri was crucial for this business transformation.

It is probably as relevant now as it was when she first implemented it some thirteen years ago.

It wasn't to last though and I was lucky, because I was attached to the Domain business line. I wasn't for the chop when the finance director inevitably went down the list at that time of the quarter when they needed to cut costs.

Liri didn't have the safety of a client paying directly for her, so in effect she was a cost to the agency. They didn't appreciate her value or allow her close enough to their clients. The bravery just wasn't there and after 18 months, she was forced to leave.

Liri Andersson is now an INSEAD visiting professor, teaching and consulting at C-Suite level for global brands through her own company called This Fluid World - exactly the space I wanted to get the agency into.

I survived another Finance Director spreadsheet cut. Someone or a few in management recognized my value at that time.

But the world was really starting to change, and the case studies were beginning to mount up proving by doing was absolutely the way forward.

Problem: Change is uncomfortable – no matter how big or small the organization is.

Solution: Implementation. Make things happen. Feel comfortable with the uncomfortable. Acceptance.

5
BIGGER BETTER STRONGER FASTER

I was feeling the rhythm of the agency more and more as each day went by. I watched, I noticed, and I made mental notes. I could see countless ways to make things better, faster, stronger. I could see so many ways to make positive change happen. I watched the many meetings, big ones, small ones and even attended some.

It is true, but we rarely practice it, that at any time, each of us has it in our individual power to seize the reigns of our own destiny and become the change-makers we all secretly want to be.

"I've searched all the parks in all the cities and found no statues of committees."
- G. K. Chesterton

For some people, being disruptive and different comes naturally. In children (me, for example) we often consider it defiance, naughtiness, bad behavior; we punish it out of them.

A large percentage of people just accept the punishment. They reform themselves into perfectly *"proper"* office workers, what we mistakenly call normal. The others don't seem at all willing to bludgeon themselves into the appropriate boxes. I was one of those.

Throughout all my life in agencies I had no choice but to be a rabble-rouser. But even for those who learnt to *"behave"* I believe we can drag them kicking and screaming back to something worthwhile. I think we can return them to something more resembling a creative human being. A starfish.

I am certain that we can get them to relearn the traits of

It is true, but we rarely practice it, that at any time, each of us has it in our individual power to seize the reigns of our own destiny and become the change-makers we all secretly want to be.

child- like curiosity and fearlessness that would make them a great intrapreneur.

We are programmed by parents and teachers to see things as right or wrong and it takes real work to reprogram ourselves out of the right/wrong mindset into the try and learn mindset.

Throughout the next fifteen years, I was to have the chance to put some of this thinking into real practice.

At my kids' school, there was a motto: *"Aut Viam Inveniam Aut Faciam."* It means *"Find a Way or Make a Way."* This really resonates with me.

My inner energy was always to just keep on pushing forward. It was relentless. Anything in my way, any seemingly immovable object became just one more reason to blow it away and get to the right result for the business.

It was never a negative energy but always a rallying call to everyone around me that things were going to happen. Watch out. As I've written in earlier chapters, this was all sparked by understanding very early on the raw power and the potential of the digital revolution. Even as I write this, we are only at the beginning of it. There's no excuse not to dive in. Nothing is fixed and even today's disruption *"du jour"* is highly likely tomorrow's legacy technology - something to be replaced.

This technology disruption was the meteor that had struck the core of our business - the TV channel. Someone had to strike back. Why not me?

Domain, my main focus area, was by now already addressing far more than just broadcast. I was starting to conceive a new way of working, almost a *"Labs"* - a new platform built on purpose to consider and then address a bewildering array of opportunity.

It seemed a simple enough idea. Take all the new things happening in our world, from streaming to gaming and from virtual reality to mobile and get everyone as excited and involved in it as possible. To use it to power us beyond the ordinary.

Then, simple to say, all we needed to do was implement it with the right partners, not just talk about it. I knew that we all needed to know and exploit it if we were to stay ahead and even drive the curve.

Because I had been sharing as much as I could with people, setting up the Lon Lab email group, I knew I was onto something, but it was all just too random.

We needed to have a proper structure and a process but one that would still allow for serendipity. *

Serendipity is a really big ally on the path - that "fortunate happenstance" or "pleasant surprise." A wonderful word and idea first coined by Horace Walpole in 1754

My answer to the need for rigor and structure was something I called the **Semesters of Learning.** Each semester was six months of intense learning on one topic.

The first one was a hot topic for many. It was becoming a big and highly misunderstood wave in the industry - streaming. To become an *"expert"* on the streaming industry, I needed to open it up, crawl all over it, and kick it to bits.

Every single week, I would see ten to fifteen different streaming companies. They would be from all around the globe. I was exhaustive in my research. I was an adrenaline-fueled detective - always on the hunt for clues. I wouldn't stop until I knew the whole crime scene.

I would contact anyone with streaming anywhere in their description. I got in touch with all the embassies and asked them to let me know anyone doing streaming in their countries. I saw them all.

I would make sure everyone had a cup of tea. I'm English.

I would give each of them 45 minutes to pitch their ideas and their company. I was in search of the best of the breed.

We were one of the world's biggest and best agencies, so we needed to work with the best partners but not just in the name. For them to get past me they also had to deliver and be hungry. They had to prove to me they really wanted to work with us. I became an expert at spotting bullshit hiding in their fancy decks. I would ask them to not talk to me like a techie, but as if I was their grandmother because if I could understand what their business was about, then I would be able to relay it to others in Ogilvy. Bringing the outside world of amazing companies inside Ogilvy. By purely knowing enough to be dangerous, my role was to start connecting the dots. I needed to look them straight in the eye. I developed a sixth sense for what they could do for us. They drank their tea. I made my choices. It worked.

I made choices based on character and intuition. I could tell who would do the business. It was in the tea leaves.

What happened next would create a bigger and bigger effect. The good people knew other good people. I wasn't messing around, people could see it was worth their while and to each semester I attached actual work. This meant developing real results for real paying clients. Our only focus was creating more and more valuable work. This stuff had to be real. It had to pay dividends.

A case in point.

The Ford chairman at the time was speaking to all his staff across the world. It was being streamed. It was a disaster. You may remember the days. It was a horror show but with real blood.

An electric storm of massive pixels obliterated everything. Every two minutes, the screen would shudder and hang. We all quickly learnt brand new words - *"pixelated"* and *"buffering"* to name but two.

During my research into streaming, I had turned up a *"startup"* from Australia called Vividas. With the most wonderful team, including the amazing Caroline Tuenissen, they had developed smart compression technologies to solve this exact problem. Put simply, they were able to live stream HD content at high quality and full screen, anywhere. It was a revelation.

The by-product of introducing these innovations wasn't just the experience alone - it gave us two new revenue streams.

1. Until this time, we had never done internal communication for Ford. We were considered their *"advertising agency,"* not

an internal communications agency. That was someone else's role.

2. And because we could actually produce the content in our own edit facility - it was a live stream to 22,000 desk tops in 19 countries in five languages. It was the TV department at Ogilvy that could charge the work.

It was yet another first. We were the ones to implement it. We did it because of a brand-new partnership with Vividas. An unknown company and startup at that time, who had nothing to do within the advertising industry.

Of course, it was painful because no one had ever done it before. It was alien to everyone around. It wasn't like doing a TV ad. Yes, we didn't know whether it would work or not and no we didn't know how to price it. We were doing it all for the first time, but something inside me knew I could trust these guys. Thankfully enough, people trusted me.

This was revolutionary because it meant that Ogilvy could now offer not just TV and print, but now live streaming. Once it had been done once, then they could offer it again and again. Simple, a new platform, technology or medium had been developed, tried, tested and produced. Something tangible that could be shown in new business meetings and credentials and most importantly to be put into the industry awards.

Ogilvy & Mather is a globally renowned brand - a major agency. David Ogilvy its founder is right regarded as a legend and father of the modern era of creative industry.

He wrote, *"advertising is a business of words, but advertising agencies are infested with men and women who cannot write. They cannot write advertisements, and they cannot write plans. They are helpless as deaf mutes on the stage of the Metropolitan Opera."*

And, *"it takes a big idea to attract the attention of consumers and get them to buy your product. Unless your advertising contains a big idea, it will pass like a ship in the night. I doubt if more than one campaign in a hundred contains a big idea."*

He stood out because he made sense. He kept it simple, real and wasn't afraid to speak the truth. He was a genuine pioneer and you could tell he was a leader because he had many followers.

People partnering with us knew that if they did a great job that it could be highly lucrative. They knew we were a red-hot reference. I made sure that they knew they were going to get supported. They would get a good case study.

They knew that would mean that they could get the funding they needed, and they could do it saying that they were working with a name like Ogilvy.

I knew there was no way that this was *not* going to work. I didn't know why, and if asked I would have had to say *"I don't know"* a million times, but that's OK. I had asked every question I could think of. I had tried to imagine all the answers I would need.

I felt as prepared as I could be to defend these ideas. I had looked at things every which way.

Isn't it funny how business people behave when they don't know the answer? What a funny little dance we do. The overly jingoistic verbiage we spout when we're trying to cover up the fact that we have no idea what's going on. Wouldn't it be amazing if more people simply had the courage to drop the act and say those three little words: *"I don't know?"*

I've never had a problem admitting I don't know something. Children ask it all the time, but we forget when we're adults. We feel that we're supposed to have all the answers. I don't, and I'm quite happy to say so. I frequently say things like, *"I don't know, but I know someone who might,"* or *"I don't know, explain it to me."*

The other insight was that people apportion blame. They do so if they don't know the answer. Then they can start shouting. My favorite saying to my team was always *"you don't know what you don't know"*. Do not be frightened to admit it. It will be our role to know the person who does know the right answer, we just need to know enough to be dangerous and then connect the dots. That is the hardest thing to measure, because intrapreneurs are connecting dots most hours of the day. It is in our DNA.

At that point I felt my role was to act as a kind of barrier to stop it. This kind of behavior got everyone nowhere at all. It scared people most of the time and they would stop showing up.

We were a brand-new team of collaborators and between us we stood up for each other. We made sure we stayed calm at all times. We would get to the finish line one small step at a time.

Many people in business, especially *"leaders"* don't ask questions. They are supposed to know. They have a real fear of failure - of losing face and not seeming smart. They're not comfortable with asking the *"thick user"* questions. As I said in the previous chapter, I am. It makes perfect sense to me.

I don't mind being a thick user. If I don't understand something, chances are that other people are confused too. You can't move forward unless you get some answers. Paralysis happens when you stop asking questions. What we were doing was asking the questions about the agency's future. We were in pursuit of better answers.

To me, this wasn't about failure; it was about learning. If the failure to face up to your own failure or vulnerability is what prevents us from moving forward, how do we become unafraid? How do we make progress? Where will the new answers come from?

I think the Israelis have it right. They are a nation constantly under threat, and because everyone goes into the army when they're 18, Israel is a nation very comfortable with the dangerous. The unknown is where we innovate. I was inspired by the book *Start Up Nation,* the story of Israel's economic miracle by Saul Singer and Dan Senor. It gave me huge insights for future leadership ideas in creating a group of intrapreneurs within Ogilvy. We initially called them *"Lab Rats"* in the early days. There was to be no ego attached, we were all the same, zero hierarchy.

When you face failure in the military context, the consequence is death. After you've gone through that, failure in business is small potatoes. There are bonds forged in fire, and that kind of brotherhood is important in the business context as well.

Each semester of learning had to have a tangible result. It wasn't a *nice to have*, it was built in. This was real work with real outcomes. It allowed us to bring fresh juice to the creative process and our product.

Domain, at this time, added value right across the piece. It was always hard to show how ideas and innovation, energy and passion, rubbed off with everyone, but everyone knew it had. Now we started building multiple case studies off the back of the approach. I didn't know it yet, but the *"Labs"* concept was getting ever closer. Momentum has its own force. Case study after case study brought new opportunities. We were getting noticed for creativity and innovation in its own right. These case studies were used for both new business purposes and to change how we were beginning to work.

Whereas, we were certainly known for globally award-winning TV and print, now we were in the new and sexy businesses of live streaming and digital distribution. It was scary.

Each semester involved a deep dive. I'd have to go to a streaming media conference and speak about what we had done. We had only just done it, so we probably hadn't even understood that ourselves. I certainly didn't know anyone there, and I didn't know anything really about this space. Plus, the people there had never heard of this *"ad agency"* startup. Initially, it was an uncomfortable environment. Extremely out of my comfort zone in those days.

And as I know now, that's where the magic happens, out of one's own comfort zone.

We had arrived in an entirely new space. A buzz was emerging. It got us into new conversations and that rippled and opened up doors for the agency that had never been opened fire. We started to get our name around the place and with new reasons to be spoken to.

It was a competitive edge and put us into a place where other agencies had never been. It gave us an amazing reputation. We were seen as a company that was not only forward thinking but being tagged as high-tech, highly creative, and doing great work.

We were building the black book of extremely exciting companies that were emerging out of this technical and digital revolution.

Throughout the semester, we would have Lab lunches where it was open for the agency and their clients or interesting ideas to be floated and conversation encouraged. At the end of the semester, we would have a Lab Day for a couple of hundred people. This gave us the chance to put together the *"best in breed"* in streaming. It was a chance for them to speak and meet their peers and our agency teams. It was an exciting space for all our clients to come along and see what we were doing in these new areas.

After streaming, I turned our focus to the *"virtual world."* At this time, there was a lot of talk about something called Second Life that came out of Silicon Valley, set up by a man called Philip Rosedale.

If it isn't broke, don't fix it - so we applied exactly the same scenario.

We did the same exhaustive testing; the deep diving into who was who in virtual worlds. We were similarly obsessively interested in what it was about. How did it work? And who was going to be interested in this technology from an advertising and media perspective?

Virtual worlds were starting to be seen as a trend at places like SXSW - which the advertising industry didn't even know about at that time, or even attend. But the high-tech press knew all about it and if it started there, then most of the time, it would reach a tipping point and reach the masses just like Facebook, Twitter, Instagram, mobile, gaming, data, and many other things did.

During this time, the creative director of the agency came to see me. He had the idea to flood Second Life to raise awareness to climate change. It was a beautiful idea, but an idea it would remain if we couldn't figure out how to make it happen. It had to happen quickly, as there was a deadline for the Cannes Lion award show that needed to be met within the week.

Originally, we were going to do this with the WWF. Initially they couldn't make it happen. They didn't actually know where to start.

Myself, and a woman named Kathryn Parsons, who founded DeCoded and Giles Ryse Jones, now working for What Three Words got together to make this happen, along with the amazing tech skills of Neil Evely, who was working in Domain. He was never scared to *"give it a go"* and push the tech boundaries. He loved solving problems like this. It's so important to surround yourself with the doers and the makers of this world, the people that make stuff happen.

As crazy as it may sound, we set about flooding Second Life - Live. We needed to do some pretty unimaginable things. This was a virtual world, but there were some very real economics and practicalities to solve. Like getting approval from Anshe Chung, known for being the first *"virtual millionaire."* She was an avatar (online personality) who owned land in the online world called Second Life. She lived in Hong Kong.

Oh - small detail - how does one actually flood a virtual world? Being an ad agency, we wanted to tell everyone about it. We wanted to do it in real time. And we didn't want anyone killed during the making of all this. Not even any virtual fish.

All of this was not something that had ever been done before. Or since to my knowledge. But that was the genius of what we could do.

Once again, nobody said we couldn't. We did it live and flooded around eight countries during the course of the day. The film was done and put up for awards. The film was then shared across social channels in the pursuit of making everyone think to make a difference and ultimately be more aware of climate change.

The agency was once again seen as forward thinking and innovative. This was never about just doing research and talking about virtual worlds because we could, it was about using new tools and techniques to make something; to create the difference for our client and the topic in general.

It was showing how a brand could make something happen that wasn't just TV or print advertising.

In the end, we were lucky that the sponsor wasn't WWF. At the last minute, they didn't seem to want to go through the pain barrier of what it would take. Eventually our client was an enormously brave guy and climate change crusader, David de Rothschild, who is a famous British adventurer.

When you're doing things like this, you need to amass lots of different people who want the same thing as each other. Let's say it's a little bit like making a cake. You need all the ingredients together to make it rise and taste good or all that hard work is for nothing.

You also quickly learn that you need small and clearly tasked teams with a clear and simple plan. You definitely do not need loads of contact reports and endless meetings. You need the right people in the right place at the right time who all want the same outcome. They need to be inspired by the challenge, ignited by the passion to innovate and sometimes do something never done before. Both Ford for streaming and Second Life for flooding won the agency many, many awards. They were great early innovation days, starting to build momentum of a world of possibility for the agency. A proven model to educate and inspire in order to innovate and complete projects never done before.

Ogilvy & Mather was rightfully getting an amazing reputation for doing interesting things in London. And now there was a global print production offering called Redworks. It seemed a natural evolution to put Domain in and create Redworks broadcast. This would be the first broadcast offering that did more than just TV. This was a completely fresh and new way to think and work.

Over the next few years, we would innovate and produce many amazing new ideas across the group. OgilvyOne was starting to see what I was doing in this space.

It was Paul O'Donnell the CEO and Mike Dodds the COO for OgilvyOne that were keeping an eye on my work and also Redworks Broadcast. I didn't know, but it was around this time, they were thinking about setting up a lab in London and there would be other labs set up around the world.

This was the period that started me thinking about future talent and more generally the future of talent. It was a constant observation of mine that the people coming through were not the types that would change the world. They wouldn't rip up trees.

In many ways, they were great and smart people, but where was the diversity, the edge, and the sparks to make something truly brilliant? The majority were white middle-class males and Oxbridge educated.

I had been moved, like many people, after seeing a talk by Sir Ken Robinson on creativity and education. It was his TEDTalk and Steve Jobs Stanford University commencement speech that did it for me. Many people saw these things, but I wanted to actually do something about it.

Here's my idea - I wanted the kids that were about to be expelled from school. I figured they had a disruptive streak, for whatever reason and if only I could channel that energy into creative and constructive outcomes I could fix this challenge for the agency and for them too. It fired me up to imagine we could do something like that and really alter lives.

I had been going through some difficulties with parenting teenagers of my own. I had a similar challenge with my own son Max. He was supremely smart but maybe not hugely academically interested enough for Oxbridge. He was a logical and divergent thinker. Yes, he was disruptive at school, but not naughty.

Like many kids, he was just questioning (in his way) everything that went on around him. He would ask why, and how come, who said so, and because of our systems and the conformity we seem to want to breed into our kids, the teachers didn't like it at all.

All they did was keep telling him he was a naughty boy. To sit down, be quiet and concentrate and focus for eight hours a day. He couldn't do that, and neither could I. It drove me to do a number of things. Push right back at the school system and tell them this was their issue and not a child that doesn't see the sense in what he's being asked to do and do something for kids who, through no fault of their own didn't see why conformity would ever get them anywhere. I had never experienced this before with my daughter.

The school hadn't often met me, as Claudia was a straight A student. She didn't question like Max did. I was to find out that her questioning would come later.

I adore my kids' sense of curiosity and the questions that makes sure it feels right in their tummies and their heads. I am extremely proud of them every day. They teach me continuously.

My insight saw that Max was actually better than fine, and it was the system that was wrong. He had talent that didn't fit the educational sausage factory.

I felt the ones that rebelled were probably more useful than the ones the machine spat out. I would be proved right, not only by Max but by all those we touched through our development of the Rough Diamond program.

This was the dawning of the intrapreneur. Some people reinvent history to make themselves feel better. If they try something and it doesn't work, they'll go to enormous lengths to cover up their failure, which really only serves to make the problem worse.

I was right at the start of building something special. It was going to need the right partnerships and the best environment for learning and support, but it would be worth it. I could feel it.

Rough Diamond, as the name suggests, was going to be a future talent platform, a program that would find kids age 14, about to be expelled and give them a lifeboat. This was something they could see, something they could really do, something that would inspire them and that they could embrace.

Now we could really problems through the forces of disruption and creativity and driven by the simple power of what's good.

This was the dawning of the intrapreneur. Some people reinvent history to make themselves feel better. If they try something and it doesn't work, they'll go to enormous lengths to cover up their failure, which really only serves to make the problem worse.

The intrapreneurial approach to trying new things is to test and learn. Try something out, even if you're not sure it will work. If it fails, don't lie about it, not even to yourself. Just try a different way next time.

There is no judgment in failure, only the opportunity to make a different choice next time.

To me that just makes perfect sense.

Problem: Sometimes, people just don't understand you or that difficult things happen

Solution: 'Aut Viam Inveniam Aut Faciam' – find a way or make a way. My kids school motto. Sometimes you just have to figure it out.

6

IT'S EASIER TO ASK FOR FORGIVENESS THAN PERMISSION

*O*K, I'm guessing by now you're beginning to see why someone like me would be branded a pain in the arse.

I cared. I was challenging the conventions and simply asking the questions that I felt would make us think. I was, after all, a rabble-rouser.

I felt it ironic that asking these questions should be our role as an agency. That this kind of challenging stance was our core role for clients, and we found it unpalatable to do it to ourselves. All I was doing seemed so simple to me. I was asking the question *"why?"* continuously.

I remember one time with Pizza Hut, a clear example of asking *"why?".* It was totally challenging the business model.

The big agencies had started to become a *"body shop"* model. It seemed to me it was very traditional thinking and made money in the usual ways. It was about employing lots of bodies to be charged to a client by the hour. The more bodies, the more money they were going to make. This was flying in the face of the increasingly popular opinion.

Agencies didn't make the kind of money they used to through production anymore, so the question was going to be how to make money. It became the strategy to have more meetings.

One meeting after another after another. That was becoming the unit of work - more bloody meetings.

Now you've got someone like me saying, *"that's a complete waste of time!"*

There's no point spending all that money doing that when you can just have a few good people with far better and more wide-scale briefs doing stuff that clients would willingly pay for. It would make everything way more efficient, far quicker, and we'll make money by doing more valuable and valued work - but in a different way. Total and utter frustration.

There must be a better way for everyone concerned.

Big agencies like to be in big buildings. It's how it's always been with the top executives in the biggest corner offices. It was about pure ego. It adds a massive overhead that the clients need to pay for, and they know it. It fosters a culture of excess and builds an entitled culture. It gives the wrong people great views over town and allows them to put the awards they had little or nothing to do with on bookcases full of books and white papers they've never read.

Now we inhabit the world of co-working spaces with technology that allows us to work from home. Big expenses like plush corner offices, are just that, big expenses!

It's a bloody catastrophe in my eyes. This isn't moving with the times. Nowadays creatives and teams can work far more productively from homes and smart hubs. The traditional agencies are promoting 20th century thinking with their predilection for glass and big headquarters.

This old model complete with enormous buildings with acres of people goes against the grain. It flies directly in the face of where the world is headed today.

Technology has been a complete game changer.

I remember with the Olympics (happening in London in 2012) we needed to work alternative hours. There was going to be major disruption with transport around our offices in Canary Wharf, London. So, I worked out with the team when their best and most productive times of the day were. Some were better in the morning, some better later in the day. Although, we were meant to only change working hours for the few weeks of the Olympics, we actually worked out our day like that always from then on. It meant that the team were always super productive working the hours that suited their personalities. It is not a *"clock on clock off"* mentality anymore based around the repetitive and soulless routine of meetings. That is where large corporates are going wrong with the *"always be at your desk mentality."*

Having worked in small tight creative agencies, the core driver is creativity and value. In these factory ships, the driver is the dollar. This means everyone's job is pulling in enormous amounts of money to keep it all going. Sadly, that means someone had to suffer. For me that meant the client and creativity, those who woke up every day to do something of actual value. Us.

Most people love big ideas, especially the ones that send shivers down your spine or that you see, could actually change the world. Nowadays there are whole conferences where people meet to talk through incredible concepts and conspire to share in their passion for change and impact. This all about making big ideas come to life. Intrapreneurs feed off this energy and the raw material of original ideas. More importantly they thrive on really getting them built and delivered. They actually love doing the messy, dirty work. Sure, things don't always work. More often than not, things don't work out. It takes an intrapreneurial spirit to keep slogging on until enough things work and are made sustainable against the constant tide of change.

Even if it doesn't work, you learn. Which is what life is about. A continuous thirst for curiosity and learning. Not to view anything as failure. Everything is a life learning. You just have to adjust your perspective.

In his article *"We don't Need More Thinkers, We Need More Doers,"* Dave Trott condemns the vast swarm of ideas, the trends, the *"coulda-shoulda-wouldas"*, and instead praises the doers, the people who have the guts to make something happen from nothing.

Just try it, what is the worst that can happen? Most are paralyzed with fear when faced with making a decision. So, they freeze and do nothing and fix another meeting.

Most creatives, he argues, are really just stylists, making things look pretty instead of inventing entirely new ways to get things done.

You see it all the time amongst the very top echelon of society, the CEOs, the Presidents, the MPs, other people write their talks. They're terrified of people finding out that they're all bluster and no action, all gong and no dinner.

They get everyone else to do everything for them, they delegate, because they have never actually delivered. Increasingly, they are getting found out. The new world is busting this superficiality, bringing a new kind of transparency and busting the myths of such bullshit. There's far fewer places for these people to hide. The power is with the people and with each and every one of our individual brand. Honesty is the new buzzword.

If not, you will be found out. There's no more hiding places when it comes to the modern world of data and social media.

The older style of leaders also tends to be the kind of people who are truly scared of innovation. These are the types who will kick out intrapreneurs when they find them. They are fearful of the risk they pose to the existing order of things. They will see innovation as a challenge to the existing systems and processes - systems and processes that they've invested millions putting in place while they've been in post.

They're also terrified to admit they don't know something. They will never want to be shown the way by the fearless or the new breed.

I see it all the time in the hiring process. The job description calls for a change agent, someone to shake things up and offer more. I get it because that's a description of me. It's even happened to me. I'm sitting there in the interview answering their questions and defining a real agent for change and *"bam!"*

Suddenly, I'm too much of a maverick for them.

These executives know they need a real innovator, but they don't know how to handle the reality of it when they meet one.

They also don't actually know how to create the kind of corporate culture within which an innovator can operate. They don't know how to help me dismantle the outdated systems and processes nor how to allocate the resources for somebody like me to flourish.

The executives may know, at a corporate level, that they need someone to create real change, but some of those executives' egos, just can't handle the maverick, the playmaker. You may already know this feeling.

There were so many times when I imagined that I would (but didn't) turn around to the executives and say, *"Hey, please relax. You can't know it all. You can't pretend you do. Get off your high horse. Come here; give me a hug. Roll your sleeves up. Say, I don't know. I've got no idea what the answer is, but we're all in it together. Let's crack on as a team."*

Although I didn't put it like that, I certainly worked as if I had.

People close to me would read the feeling in my eyes and they would share in my pain. In some way we would console each other that we weren't the insane ones.

Eventually those like us were by far the majority. It didn't make me feel good that the famous agencies and large organizations were becoming outlived and outperformed by the smarter and more relevant alternatives in the market. It was merely a sad and (very) avoidable fact.

Because the corporate structure is inherently resistant* to intrapreneurial thinking, even when they know they need it, the intrapreneur has really only two avenues. One is getting enough buy-in to sustain a project, and the other is doing the thing anyway. *(Note: * This is also relevant with our education system - it is a model that is "broadcast at" - so any child challenging the status quo, is seen as "naughty." Hence the need to create "the Rough Diamond" future talent program.)*

Ideally the two must work in tandem, and in some situations, it would call for one over the other, but together, they give the intrapreneur the space to create change even in an environment that is highly likely to be resistant to it.

To some extent, there just isn't a palatable way forward if the whole organization is averse to change. You have to pray that there are one or two people at the top who are willing to engage properly in the new ideas.

When this happens, you have to quickly show them a few wins and then they'll really come on board. You have to pick the ones with the pull to bring other executives on board with them.

At a certain point, the intrapreneur decides to ask for forgiveness, not permission. You make something happen without waiting for the OK, and then you say, *"See? Look what I did!"* And with luck they say, *"Oh, ok, fine, I get it."* I'm a firm believer in *"asking for forgiveness and not for permission."*

I will always remember one of my very first talks at the Direct Marketing Awards. The award organizers were very specific. They wanted me to speak about being the *"disruptive one"* at Ogilvy. They wanted me to be the last presenter so that I could give a crunchy, thought-provoking speech. I knew there were going to be a lot of Ogilvy Business Directors there, but I also knew there would be a lot of clients, so I planned accordingly.

I've always been authentic and honest.

I couldn't get up on stage and sugar coat anything, and I genuinely wanted to deliver a deeply loyal talk about my agency. I didn't try to hide anything. Indeed, I sent a copy of my presentation to a few senior executives. I gave my talk, in an open, honest fashion.

I talked truthfully about how Ogilvy wasn't actually giving me any money for R&D or all this innovation gathering and input. I said I had found a workaround to that which made us all happy by raising money from Rory Sutherland's speeches. I got great feedback from the clients there. I got calls and emails telling me how my talk had given clients a lot to think about regarding how to be creative about where money can be found and how that in itself was innovation.

The next morning, I got a call from the Managing Director.

He said, *"I've never been so embarrassed in my whole life."* I told him I was busy, and we'd have to talk tomorrow. That gave him some time to calm down, and it gave me time to get my ducks in a row.

He was really upset, and I was upset that he was feeling so disappointed that I'd aired *"dirty laundry"* in public. To him, I'd let clients know that the agency wasn't funding R&D. I talked him down and explained that was all OK and it was innovation and how to work with more effective business models.

In the end he could only tell me off for a couple of points on my delivery.

This was a moment of change, it signaled a move away from *"smoke and mirrors" and "dark art."* It called for us to be open and honest about genuine change and address the actual problems. It heralded collaboration with people who could find fresh and possible alternative solutions. It suggested a time when we should all actually help each other and not drive blindly off the cliff of inevitability.

Nothing changed here of course. But the whole episode taught me two things.

It brought home the extent of the bubbles in people's heads. The echo-chambers we hear so much about these days. The close-mindedness to new thinking. The grasping on to legacy thinking. It was symptomatic of the dirty little secrets at the top of many corporate hierarchies.

It also taught me that I was experiencing a massive shift.

I was starting to feel a sea change in the business world as a whole. There was a hunger for innovative thinking, a desire to do things differently and a need for transparency and honesty within the corporate world.

My intrapreneur was born and being tested as I knew it would be. I wasn't for giving up any time soon.

The below is the intrapreneur Chris Denson's, (Founder of Innovation Crush and author) point of view as to how he found my "weirdness."

This Is Your Mentor Moment

True innovation is a holistic practice. It's not simply something you do. It's something you live, breath, and is exhibited through craft. It's the way an artist sees a painting before the first brush stroke. It's the way a songwriter hears a melody before her fingers touch a single key, or an architect who has the building complete in his mind before a single drop of ink touches the draft board.

As their careers and crafts evolve, these visionaries learn to leave room for improvisation and the unexpected, and leverage both to create masterpieces; each one often better than the last. In the same vein, a true innovator sees a forthcoming beauty of culture, business and technology just a split second before the rest of us; and harnesses it to create something wonderful. In that vain, Nicole Yershon is a true innovator.

I first met Nicole after I left a company I had been working for and began looking to expand my horizons within the innovation economy. At that time, I was somewhat unfulfilled and had envisioned myself as some form of misfit toy.

Sure, I was fun, and shiny, and smart, and eager to play. But for some reason, I didn't seem to match up correctly with the rest of the other toys I had been put in the box with; and as such, felt my potential was also somewhat trapped in that box as well. After some growing professional discomfort, I set out to find a remedy.

Like an orphan who was finally ready to know who I really was, I sought out different organizations and individuals to connect with and learn more about corporate Labs, and incubators, and the individuals who made them work. At the time (and still at the time this book was ready to print), there wasn't a lot to choose from and reach out to. The mere fact that despite living in one of the most creative cities on the planet, my cold email had to be sent clear across the world speaks volumes to that point.

Not only had Nicole gotten my email and taken the time to write back to some American weirdo, she even went as far as setting up a call. Knowing her now, it's the combination of curiosity and generosity that she exhibits in her work that also echo in her approach to embracing new people and experiences. All essential tools in the innovator's toolbox. During our two-hour, long distance call, she and I chatted about almost everything that's captured in this book.

Up until that conversation I had never heard the word "intrapreneur," let alone conversed on concepts like corporate support, emotional intelligence, internal education, structured innovation, and the like. She talked about the uphill battles faced. She talked about the successes her company enjoyed because of her ability to withstand those battles. She talked about Rough Diamonds, relationships, work-life balance and knowing her and her teams' value. She talked about being an irresistible force against immovable objects.

She didn't however, talk about offering me a job - which was kind of my underlying hope! But that's part of the journey. Sometimes information is more important than opportunity.

By the time we got off the phone, I felt like Bruce Willis' character at the end of The Sixth Sense. Nicole was Haley Joel Osmet, seeing things in the world no one else saw, and I was a ghost who suddenly saw everything he had had gone through from completely a different point of view.

Everything I had felt and experienced and struggled with understanding in my professional journey, she articulated with undeniable clarity during that conversation. And I was now free to embrace this new information and move on to whatever was next for me.

Therein lay the purpose of this book. I've never had a mentor. At least not some guru I visit or call on a regular basis to go over my life with. Rather, I refer to what I like to call "mentor moments," - brief encounters with people who have an experience or perspective that either affirms or enhances the path you're on. Sometimes it's a chat during a networking mixer. Other times it's something you hear someone say in a meeting. And sometimes, it's a phone call you take with someone in London while wandering the streets of West Hollywood on foot.

'Mentor moments' - brief encounters with people who have an experience or perspective that either affirms or enhances the path you're on.

Over the years, Nicole has become a dear friend, collaborator, professional confidant and a voice of inspiration. Whether we connect at conferences, in either of our home countries, or over a quick WhatsApp chat, the conversations always offer enlightenment, encouragement, inspiration, and some friendly competition.

I feel like this book is one of our conversations. It's her truth, experience, and wisdom all captured over the course of 70,000 some words.

Shortly after our first phone call, I decided to create Innovation Crush, an interview series dedicated to profiling some of the best innovators around the globe. I wanted to reveal to the world some of the methodologies and thinking behind how innovation comes to life. Inviting Nicole to be a guest was a decision I made without hesitation. I knew my audience needed her voice. She was my seventh episode and was recorded on my second day of production. To this day, her interview remains one of the top ten listened to episodes in the history of the show.

What Nicole happens to help us work through is that in some way, shape or form, we're all misfit toys waiting to find a home that appreciates us. We're all artists in our own right, waiting for our unique vision to come to life.

The universal truth is that we're all striving to be our highest self. Be it a collective self in the form of a company, or simply understanding what role our individual self plays in the innovation ecosystems we're a part of. When it comes to understanding how to go from here to there, Nicole's words are now mentorship moments in print. Read them with care. Share them with others. Put them to good use.

Problem: People will often say no, or that it cannot be done

Solution: Ask for forgiveness and not for permission.

7
HUNTING WITH HUNTERS

I had to go and look this word up.

Many years ago, Marc Lewis the Dean of the School of Communication Arts in London, told me he thought I was an *"intraprenuer."*

At first I thought it was another made up jargon word and I just looked blankly at him. Wikipedia calls it like this:

"Intrapreneurship is the act of behaving like an entrepreneur while working within a large organization. Intrapreneurship is known as the practice of a corporate management style that integrates risk-taking and innovation approaches, as well as the reward and motivational techniques, that are more traditionally thought of as being the province of entrepreneurship."

WOW, they've got a name for me. I loved it. Perhaps I wasn't alone.

I had been brought into this global agency because of my crazy passion for doing stuff. Actually, getting things done. I was known for adding value. My obsession was creating impact, even though there was risk. Changing things always has risk. Not changing things usually carries greater risk!

Around this time, I was also beginning to see that there was a difference between my definitions of things and others. I was that square peg in a round hole. I was humble enough to know I was no better than anyone else, yet wise enough to know I was different.

Value Is In The Eye Of The Beholder

OK, so I messed with that phrase a bit. But some days I felt I was fighting a rearguard battle with those that I assumed saw the value. People would say, *"I thought Nicole was an ad person. What's she doing milling around with all these 'below the line' people?"*

An ad person? This was a big moment for me. It showed me that status really was a thing and not always a good thing and that people were genuinely scared of things *"being"* different. I began to see that they didn't want to be shown a new way to think and work. They just saw a threat to their positions and their way of life.

I had heard the cliché. I knew that change was never ever welcomed, but this was the first time in my life that some of the *"old guard"* were actively going to be a problem. Even worse, some of the leaders of the business, those who I had assumed brought me in to do just this, found it really difficult to *"get it."*

I was proud to be a part of it all but was starting to feel questioned about the value that I was bringing. It was OK in the early days. My natural style was to just keep pushing and believing that I could get them across the line.

It was a mammoth undertaking. Over ten years we conducted two semesters of learning each year every six months - which I cover in later chapters! We researched gaming, mobile, streaming, virtual worlds, augmented reality, music, big data, behavioral change, startups, future retail, future travel and tourism and many more. Because this was for consumption by a variety of audiences, we created case studies to show people how we could make innovation happen.

I put it like this:

Problem: When an organization can't do everything themselves, how do you partner and collaborate to future proof your organization?

Solution: Semesters of Learning.

The Age Of The Super Connector

I am a creative, an innovator, connecting stuff to other stuff. Making one plus one equal six. I was driven by ingenuity and finding more innovative solutions to help creative executions and ideas. Like all creatives I guess - I do this by spotting something unique in the chaos of things. I put myself into a *"superconnector"* role. I spot a something, for example, something that's being done in VR, a key person. I spot, I connect, I create. I identify potential.

Connecting things is crucial. Connecting them fast is a competitive advantage. New things happen to us every day, new products, new ideas, new technologies and new relationships.

Some make us better, others trip us up. Some we call innovation some we call disruption. We wake up, we see and hear all the new stuff - tons of fresh data that comes into our world. That's what informs us.

We often say, *"we know what we know"* and *"we don't know what we don't know."* The fact is what we know may not be the best knowledge and what we don't know might be massively more valuable. So how do we get to know what we *should* know and in time for it to help us?

If you think about it, we don't really need more *"things."* We just need the *right* "things". People are brilliant at making new *"things"* all the time. We live in an age of immense "thingness." The biggest thing about *"things"* is there's too many. What's crucial is to choose which *"things"* are important. That often means finding out the *"thing"* is even there.

Our challenge is finding them, knowing which of them matter and are we sure they are of the most value. How do we find out about *which* things and *why* these things are the right things and then making them the most valuable for us.

A connector does that. They connect. They know what's out there, they know who is doing what, they know who needs what and then they connect.

Over the years I developed and continue to refine my eye for talent. I seem to have an instinct to understand people's character. I'm constantly filtering. I do it in every conversation I have. I develop a framework in my mind, and it guides what I'm looking for - no matter what the topic.

- Are we going to be able to work together, collaborate and pull in the same direction?
- Are we likely to trust and respect each other?
- Do we share a belief system and values?
- Is our energy and passion aligned and do we have a common language between us?

I can see things holistically and draw my own patterns and observations to identify problems or trends. It's about having that vision and knowing you will get there someway in some shape, somehow. I innovate by *"spotting,"* connecting, and then creating a basis upon which we can build - so that things actually happen.

To understand *"spotting"*, we need to go back to the semesters of learning which are key to how it works. Semesters are the process I built to *"deeply know"* something.

It's six months of intense learning on a topic. I'll talk to ten or fifteen different companies in a sector every single week. I'll go to events, i'll do some judging. I scour the world and put it out there that this is the topic I'm looking at. I find the problems that need solving, and then the solutions that need knowing. It will always exist within the space somewhere.

Then I'll implement it. I've always got an eye out for the ultimate test - a tangible case study. All the time you're sharing knowledge and you're connecting. Then at the end of the process you can put it all together in some form for people to network amongst, for speakers to speak at, for people to exhibit.

The beautiful thing is that once you start out on such an open-minded road, then serendipity starts to play. Serendipity plays a crucial role. You might call it fate - it just happens - that's a fact.

It became the highly immersive way to EDUCATE and INSPIRE in order to INNOVATE. Those three words became the Ogilvy London Labs strapline.

The fact is it was always about identifying the challenge and turning it into an opportunity. I built a place and space where connection would flourish. The challenge could be about anything.

"I want to do something more innovative in the logistics space," or *"I want to speak to consumers in their homes,"* or *"I'm looking for a talented UX person."* There are a million things that I'm connecting so that the right results would emerge. It was always about creating a result - something tangible. It was never just talk.

The Emotional Quotient

Someone sent me an email saying, *"I need someone who can talk about emotional intelligence."* It was a topic that I needed to know a lot more about.

Whatever topic I was called on to help with, I knew just enough to be smart about it but more than enough to know where it needed to play. I became the *"expert generalist."* The key then was to know the right person to go deeper - the one who knows way more than me.

And it was where my *"Black Book"* came into play. My bank where I kept information of every single company and each great person I have met along the journey. By combining these resources and understanding the challenge fully it enabled me to solve for anything and make it all manageable at the same time.

Innovation was always about being ingenious and creative with time and resources, connecting the dots, creating the safe space and allowing the magic to happen.

When people talk about innovation, they just want to talk about the top bit, but they fail to see all the underneath bits, what goes into it - the Semesters of Learning. You can't just magic up innovation. You can't just name someone the *Head of Innovation* and expect innovation, which is different thinking.

There's a schism in how the agency world gets seen by the clients and the wider industry. Over the years it has shifted and evolved but not much. There used to be what was known as *"above"* and *"below the line."* Above was the ads and the *"big print"* that was needed for outdoor posters and below was everything else - direct mail and all that. Below was definitely the second-class citizen.

It often gets described through the iceberg metaphor. Nowadays all of the work below the surface is what forms the customer experience and what customers see and touch because of the digitization and smarts. It's turned the iceberg on its head. Adverts and posters are still a part of it and very important but it's still just one small part.

The trouble is above and below are two very different religions and back then they were at war. I was in the middle - part protagonist and part terrorist.

During this time, I had an even bigger problem to solve. The work that was necessary to be done beneath the surface (for innovation to occur) was hard enough. Harder still was to change the attitudes and cultures of the tip of the iceberg. That's where all the leaders went for glory - it was how they were all measured, in KPIs (key performance indicators). It was the stuff that traditionally got talked about and was very glamorized within the media world. This needed to change if we were to survive.

It was difficult to make middle management see. It was a deeply frustrating time. Surely, they could see where the world was going and ignoring the rich opportunity of the whole iceberg seemed utter insanity. Thank goodness for at least some *"buy in"* at the top for 16 years.

Everybody gets caught up on words. All the things that happened below the surface were important to make the stuff above work. They both worked together. They both needed doing. But they undervalued the doing. I needed to figure out why it flew past their ears and noses.

The gap in the understanding started to show up in some pretty graphic ways.

Imagine a scenario where the CEO of a company shows up to an event to talk about the launch of their new smart phone. The CEO is responsible for the work of many thousand people. Everyone at the event asks the CEO about everything but the phone.

"Tell us more about all the innovation going on and all stuff that we see here - that's way more interesting."

That was what it was like. All the clients could see the innovation at my events or going on in the marketplace and didn't want to talk about the traditional bits any longer. I was the subject of scorn at times and not the object of value that most everyone else could see. My growing frustration with the attitude of the leaders was heightened because although they would make it personal I never thought it was about me or this role.

In those days I was very happy to be a cog in their wheel.

I always wanted the agency and the leadership to get the glory. These were difficult and frustrating times. They were times when others may well have given up or looked elsewhere.

The middle management seemed disinterested and dismissive of the very thing they said they had bought into and should be leveraging. But success was always measured by the dollar, the day job always seemed to get in the way. My work was often viewed as peripheral. It was described by those who should have known better as the *"nice to have,"* pink and fluffy stuff, but it really wasn't. Innovation is necessary for the future.

It's a common malaise in business that the system and the culture closes rank on what's new because it smells of risk and change. It shocked me that this could happen in a creative agency. A type of business that's supposed to take all the change and disruption going on and eat it for breakfast.

On one memorable occasion there was a Survey Monkey done to the Executives. I didn't deal with them that often but fair enough. My work was with the people on the shop floors, the doers.

One of the survey questions was, *"what should the lab stop doing?"* They said, *"stop going to SXSW (South by Southwest)."*

I insisted the survey go out to the people that were doing actual work, those who we were working with on a daily basis. The disparity between what they felt and what the doers felt was unbelievable.

The executives were clinging on to what they were used to seeing and happy to measure. They were comfortable and safe in the traditional - the fetishized tip of the iceberg. I was shocked by their lack of appreciation of what was required by our clients and what we actually did to bring the much-needed value about.

A common misconception of innovation is that people only see the end result of it. Clearly that end result is the culmination of a huge process. It's the distillation of what's survived a rigorous process - and then gets pushed out into the world.

People see the end result, and they think it's an easily repeatable process. You expect consumers to ignore what it takes to build that car (for example) but you expect the leaders to value the supply and manufacturing chain that made the car and made the industry possible.

Enlightened executives know that innovation is an integral part of survival in today's world. They know that a vibrant, dynamic company, and the supportive culture is vital to make it happen. But in a failing enterprise, it's often misunderstood and understood way too late to be able to fix it.

On the other hand, executives don't understand innovation, but they do understand that they need to allow it to flourish. And there are others still who are only interested in where it hits the bottom line. The creative process doesn't help. It isn't a standard time and materials thing. It just isn't. Creativity happens in the shower at 6:30am and maybe it wins an award three to six months later. Or it takes three months to gestate and frustrates the hell out of everyone. Executives have never really understood how to cope with that.

Finance departments have always had a problem with creative departments, and now they had to face up to the crazy *"Head of Disruption."* This wasn't going to end well. The creative process is never happy to be in bondage to the timesheet.

Time and again there were gunfights and showdowns over allocating any budgets for innovation. My role started to be as much about finding the people who cared passionately about this kind of stuff as it was about mining for innovation myself. But the role of an intrapreneur is to *"Find a way and make a way"*. So moving forward is what was always needed, or else, you're going backwards (as my Dad always likes to remind me).

It was about forcing people to get out more, to go to different events, to bring outside information in, understand and then distribute it within their teams.

Executives were also very slow to appoint people from a different tribe. They didn't know how to cope with or manage the more natural creatives, the new hunters, the people who would infiltrate innovation in the right way and share all the information they found out about it.

What can I say? We were trouble-makers, the ones the teachers didn't like at school because we were always questioning authority, asking about doing it another way. And of course, none of that feels particularly constructive or controllable to senior managers.

I always felt they needed to relearn how to measure innovation. They were miles away from understanding the real value. When I talk about value, I mean the more intangible stuff that clients see as important and not just set the KPI on revenue and dollars.

They completely missed the value of someone going to SXSW (South by Southwest). They missed the idea of a really smart way of rocket propelling themselves up the curve of what's really going on. They missed the idea of harvesting all the learning, making it consumable and valid in the creative process, bringing it back in and sharing it with the eager creatives and bringing relief to those who could see it coming.

Innovation, Technology and The Democratization Of Access

Creativity has changed so much as a result of new technology. It was always a significant investment and cost to do TV press and posters. Technology happened, consumers expectation and new capability happened. Mobile happened. Everything happened. To some leaders it was more like what the fuck happened!

We have to remember never to use technology for its own sake and always remember that we're human beings. Technology needs to be relevant and useful if it is to add any value.

There are a million examples of things we didn't have before. We didn't have augmented reality before, we didn't have digital moving posters, we didn't have the whole iceberg.

It's always amazed me to sit and watch the kids do things naturally and easily with this stuff. It disappoints me that the leaders of creative businesses don't get off on it, although I do sometimes empathize, I've never got into Snapchat!

Surely they would see that they needed to embrace some of what disruption means. The young kids from Ravensbourne College, (see Chapter 12) could do something incredibly simple such as create an app that would change how people could consume advertising. Surely, we should find out about that and learn from it?

I was beginning to feel a clash of mindsets and it was seeping into everything we were trying to achieve. It was increasingly making what should be about *"creating value"* into a battle - constantly defending innovation. Mad.

Innovation has a major impact on business and the commercial models. The ad industry is no exception. How arrogant of us to think we couldn't be touched by it and eventually sidelined. That's the brutal beauty of technological advances. We can't stop them, but we do need to embrace them.

I learnt that while creating Domain. Technological advances cover every single aspect of life and they affect all businesses. We have to accept that our world is now one of continuous change.

I remember saying years ago and to anyone who would listen:

"You can't continue forever charging this amount of money, because someone down the road will do it for a hundred quid."

Not surprisingly, I couldn't get anyone to listen or look seriously at different business models and move with the times. And in 2016 the *"Big 4"* agencies were subpoenaed for dodgy or sharp practice when it came to production cost.

I know there's far more to it than this, and I can make a counter argument of course, but just to ram home my point:

It's completely possible to pay one company $10,000 to design a logo, and at the same time spend less than $100 to get numerous ideas with unlimited revisions online without meeting a human being. Even more so when AI & Machine learning kick in.

The big companies won't consider doing it the new way. It's too much of an attack on the pricing model they wish to defend. On top of that, there are shareholders to keep happy each quarter and make the numbers they've come to expect.

A bigger question right now is how companies are ever going to be able to do that, while still looking at innovating or disrupting themselves. There is not an easy answer. I understand, but for the leaders to not look and learn from these concepts actually worries me. This was my life back then - simply challenging ourselves to innovate before we became irrelevant.

Problem: The old business model is broken.

Solution: Find the Rough Diamonds. The entrepreneurial spirits.

8

I'M MAKING IT UP AS I GO ALONG

I think most Rough Diamonds have some sense that they are different, even if they haven't heard the term. You can spot them by their attitude and by a natural ability to add controversy to a seemingly ordinary situation. That's because they've learnt that *ordinary* situations don't exist and to an intrapreneur they spell danger.

Quite simply, what exists needs to be tested for relevance and what needs to exist is going to be uncomfortable because we've never been there before.

What we learnt in the past and what we will need to survive in the future are two very different things. Lessons from the past are not determinant of the future.

History can teach though. We always need to remember that just because something worked in the past it may not in the future. And just because something didn't work in earlier circumstances doesn't mean it won't work today.

Our attitude to thinking and solving things today has to be dynamic. It must be a mix of openness, adaptability, flexibility, curiosity, thoughtfulness, and bloody-minded pragmatism or it won't work.

To really be able to deliver, I rely on my weapons grade honesty.

"Forget about the past. It does not exist, except in your memory.
Drop it. And stop worrying about how you're going to get through
tomorrow. Life is going on right here, right now
— pay attention to that and all will be well."
- Neale Donald Walsh

So, now I have left Ogilvy & Mather London advertising. I was asked to move to a group role, and mainly working with OgilvyOne with a total of 1800 people in the London office. Overall there were ten marketing communication companies in the group.

The idea was simple. To bring everything I had been doing and make it work for all of them. Paul O'Donnell and Mike Dodds were running OgilvyOne at the time with backing from Mike Walsh. He ran the group in London and they knew what I had been doing in Redworks Broadcast. I had also had some wonderful backing from Patou Nuyteman and a few global digital leaders around the network, including, OgilvyOne's global CEO, Brian Fetherstonhaugh. We went to Arizona alongside the OgilvyOne board meeting.

Together with five other countries and their people, we discussed the concept of doing *"Labs"* in each region. London for EMEA. New York, Singapore, Brazil and Beijing.

The OgilvyOne global board had asked us to figure out what the lab was for. We needed to figure out how it should look, how it would act, how much it would cost to implement, who would be part of it. We designed it from the ground up.

We were asked lots of questions over the three days of their board meeting. I was the only one there from a traditional ad agency. To be surrounded by the direct team at OgilvyOne was a very different environment for me. I was able to meet many of the global leaders running OgilvyOne, including Patou Nuyteman, who was working with Paul O'Donnell pushing the digital agenda.

Finally, we presented our thoughts as it all came to a conclusion.

Success - everyone bought into it. It was the right way to go and the timing sounded exactly right. But, as with all my experiences with these things the reality soon hit. I was probably the least surprised person there. There was no budget!

Naturally, there was a hint of disappointment from other people. But on the plane journey home I was excited. I knew Paul O'Donnell, Mike Dodds, and Rory Sutherland would allow me to be a maverick. It would turn out that Paul and Rory would give me unconditional backing for many more years, until a new CEO in the London Group would take over.

I thought and would eventually say to them that it didn't matter if I don't have any budget as long as I have your buy-in and support.

I'm simply going to magic something out the air. It is going to be amazing. I don't actually know how I'm going to do it, but I'm sure I'll make it work. Just trust me, be honest, let's keep the levels

> I'm simply going to magic something out the air. It is going to be amazing. I don't actually know how I'm going to do it, but I'm sure I'll make it work. Just trust me, be honest, let's keep the levels of communication always open and don't expect any PowerPoint presentations.

of communication always open and don't expect any PowerPoint presentations.

Before the OgilvyOne board meeting in Arizona, there had been several interesting initiatives into these territories around the world. In particular, a gentleman named Mark Seeger, doing some interesting things in Singapore Technology wise.

Brian Fetherstonhaugh thought it would be a good idea for the OgilvyOne offices globally to have a differentiator. The whole point being to set them apart from other agencies.

It was a completely rational idea - rather than everyone coming up with different ideas to solve different client's problems, we could pool all the innovation and learning and make it available across the group.

A client and team working to solve a situation in one area would immediately benefit another somewhere else.

So here we were putting all our ideas together in a way we thought would work best and we presented them.

Every month, once a month we shared progress and we continued for a couple of years. This was run initially by Patty Lyon and Mish Fletcher, who were always so supportive of this initiative. The labs in New York, being run then by Maria Mandel, Beijing, with Sascha Engle, London and Paris by David Raichman who were all totally on board. Cape Town would come on board later with Chris Rawlinson.

The labs had to all be self-funding. As time went by the London Lab seemed to be the only one that was progressing. By now I was also doing work with Ogilvy in Australia. I had started to go around the world sharing the Lab ethos. Athens in Greece, Lisbon, sessions in parts of Russia. Wherever I had a talk in the world I would drop into the local OgilvyOne office and talk to them about the Labs.

It was inspiring all round and many great people were involved. They could see and feel the value in these exchanges. No matter what they were doing, the case studies and the approach was always relevant. Taking anything that we were doing and applying relevant aspects to them and their client's assignments.

The Labs were a perfect platform at so many levels. It allowed for us to work as a network. We shared experiences, we all made much more meaningful connections, and we started to understand each other's contexts.

Getting out there and meeting at their offices sent very strong messages and helped with many of the intangible values of being a network. In practical terms, it saved us time and money too. Ordinarily, it would've taken much longer to achieve what we did without access to the right people in the right markets. With these connections we could get things done really quickly.

Eventually most of the other Labs closed for one reason or another. Funding needed to be found, the people involved needed to battle to keep their facilities in difficult economic times. The London Lab was really the last fully functional one.

Once back from Arizona, I went to work with grit and determination. It was just myself and an amazing assistant named Joanne Bloom. We were an incredible little team. It was back to being a startup.

I was in my element. It was just the two of us against the world. Like two Navy Seals on a mission we rolled our sleeves up, got serious and made something. At first, we probably didn't know what that was, but it just felt right.

Off the back of some of the jobs that we done recently in Redwood Broadcast we invented things.

That was it. We set up Ogilvy Labs in London.

Like all these things it was always going to be a work in progress, but that's no use if you want something to be consumed and real enough to attract customers. Although we were making it up as we went along, we knew our vision was for multiple audiences and a wide array of solutions and deliverables. We would need to market it.

That meant being clear enough about what it did, what it was, what it wasn't and what it meant for different audiences at different times.

I knew that until we explained it our way everyone would have had a totally different idea and I would end up going mad. Listening to everybody's different understanding of the word *"Lab"* would have created a monster.

I just thought, *"I'm not listening to anyone but myself. I'll just keep going in one direction and then at least we would get a prototype lab stood up."*

I was bringing all my experience to this party. I knew the Semesters of Learning would be key. I knew being a cost and not a profit center would be a problem, so we needed to fix for that. I knew we needed to develop something fast. I needed to develop some kind of tangible measure of success that would make real business sense.

In this world it's suicide to be a cost on that spreadsheet. If that was the case it would only be a matter of time before they would get rid of me.

However, the make-up of a maverick is to challenge what's happening, spot the stupid stuff, and do things different and better. I was always hunting the hunters, people who would be as hungry as us for value and impact. It was always a fine line, but in those early years OgilvyOne always gave me the right support at the top.

I asked Rory Sutherland to be my first revenue stream. I noticed he was an exceptional speaker. Really exceptional and engaging.

At that time, he was not really on the speaker circuit. I asked him if I could effectively act as his agent. This meant we would get money for him to speak.

Initially we did a TEDTalk. That got Rory on the map. After that, everyone wanted him to speak. There's always plenty of events, and Rory can literally make any topic sound incredibly interesting, funny, and supremely insightful.

I could charge him to speak. There was my revenue stream. I just needed to ring-fence it. I asked if we could keep any money coming from his talks and put it directly into the labs.

We could then use it for R&D to do the things I wanted to do. It was agreed, and so Rory was our first revenue stream. There would be many more.

My journey and all my lessons could have been drawn from any industry - but advertising it was. Like all industries, advertising has been attacked with some pretty serious questions about its business model and its integrity. The honesty of those involved have long been in question.

I think what made my journey an exciting and challenging one is that I've lived it based on honesty. Extreme honesty. It hasn't always made me popular to everyone, but at least I've got stuff done.

The path to a better life lies through honesty. It sounds good and true. I firmly believe it. I know how hard people try and yet fail to apply it in their

Imagine being really honest with yourself. It cuts through a lot of the usual sandbagging and all the play acting that goes on in every meeting in any industry.

lives. I hear people say that they believe it, but they can't put it into practice.

Imagine being able to be really honest with someone. Imagine being really honest with yourself. It cuts through a lot of the usual sandbagging and all the play acting that goes on in every meeting, in any industry. If I hadn't have been honest not much of the above would have happened.

I could never put up with dishonesty anyway. It drives me crazy to waste my time and those I represent going through the stupid dance. An intrapreneur has to work based on honesty.

For me, the moment I knew I was an intrapreneur was when I flooded Second Life.

That's when I realized I had this unique ability to make shit happen in weird ways. I realized I was the kind of person that people would always want to bring their weird ideas too. I was already building a reputation as someone who would turn dreams into reality. If they told me what they really wanted and worked honestly with me I would work honestly right back.

From that Second Life experience, I began to consciously act as an intrapreneur. I'd tell new joiners that my door was open, and if they were feeling brave, they'd bring me their ideas.

One of the UX (User Experience) guys, William Godfrey, came to me and said, *"I've got a weird idea."* I thought it was genius, and I marched him down to the Creative Director's office, and I introduced them, and something great was born.

At its heart, the power of the intrapreneur is to consciously create legitimate connections between people, across industries, and across hierarchies, then move on. This award-winning idea was only able to be created by knowing who to speak to make it happen. As well as an urgent want from everyone involved, including Exterion Media, to change how their digital posters interacted with people.

Whereas some people spend their whole lives in one industry, the intrapreneur consciously breaks through. They smash the silos, they establish the best connections and then they deliver the benefits of those connections to their clients and their entire companies.

Being at liberty to be a maverick - an intrapreneur - every day was exciting. That's because every day was a challenge. Never was one day the same as another. As new semesters of learning happened every six months it felt like I was always starting a brand-new job. Twice a year I'd start with a blank slate.

Many people might find that really uncomfortable. That's what drove me. I couldn't bear a situation where I would speak to the same people, go to the same events turn the same cogs and solve the same problem every day.

I'm not happy being in the same rut week after week. I'm not happy living in a clique. I'm open minded, open hearted. I listen and my mind races. The computer in my head is making calculations and conclusions and then firing rocket propelled grenades at them until a better idea survives. Yes, it quite a dangerous place inside my head.

If you want to know everyone quickly, and then become important you need to be open and honest. As long as you stay there it's a rapid path to knowing if there's value. I start with the premise that everyone is a potential connection. This way, through honesty, I soon find out if there isn't.

It's a sad reflection on business but true. Far too many people in corporate culture feel constrained, silenced or emaciated, that there's no room for innovation or creative thinking.

Academia and corporate culture effectively squash creative thinkers so that most innovators end up starting their own businesses, or if they do go into corporate, they're stymied, silenced or even fired.

So how does an intrapreneur survive when corporations are reluctant to devote any significant budget to real innovation. The intrapreneur is on their own to find the money, the resources and the connections to make things happen. Luckily, any intrapreneur worth their salt, by their very nature, will know exactly how to do just that.

Intrapreneurs get shit done. They develop a reputation for it, and soon enough that reputation brings in new connections as well as other people with the same spirit. A virtuous cycle.

Intrapreneurs are fearless, disruptive and by definition naughty. Intrapreneurs are able to deal with ambiguity

> Intrapreneurs get shit done. They develop a reputation for it, and soon enough that reputation brings in new connections as well as other people with the same spirit. A virtuous cycle.

and uncertainty. That's the whole of our art. We can walk in both worlds - the normal and the scary unknown near future. We delight in thinking grand, lofty thoughts, broad ideas. But we also delve into the details in a very granular way. And all with a strong hold on where the future is pulling us.

Questioning everything. When it came to new partnerships I became the thick buyer. I got it to the point where there wasn't any complicated legal jargon to be signed. I hated all the claptrap, forms and processes that meant nothing at the end of the day. I worked with simple MOUs (memorandum of understanding). The legal jargon just got in the way of making things happen. All the contractual stuff was made super simple. One page only that everyone understood.

The traditional problem that no one questioned was driven by the fear of being sued. I not only questioned it, but made up new rules to protect every side fairly but didn't baffle and blind everyone with bullshit.

Don't be shoehorned into making a decision just because it inconveniences someone else.

Takeaway for reader: *Don't sign what you don't understand.*

Innovation happens naturally within small companies. For example, a friend of mine runs a start up. Rather than taking two months of desk space at a WeWork and because she can't afford to pay her team bonuses, she's taking ten of them to Bali for two months, and they're working out of there.

They're staying in two separate villas, and they've got staff and people for the same amount of money it would cost in London to rent desk space.

She has the emotional intelligence to understand what drives people, and she's giving them a different balance in life.

Another example is a company I've worked with in Dorset. They've got something called Remote Working Year, which allows employees on the scheme to work remotely for a year, every month in a different country. There are 75 employees who all work from different countries. One month in Marrakesh, one month in Sofia, one month in Rio. They work in WeWork spaces and they start to connect with other companies too. To stay connected, with their original employeers they'll have a monthly breakfast together via Facetime/Skype using streaming technology despite being anywhere and everywhere.

These smaller companies are open-minded and openhearted to new ways of working. Magic definitely happens.

Intrapreneurship and institutionalizing the thought of *"why not?"* means it's probably easier to innovate at a smaller company, but it's not impossible at a large one. The value is so disproportionate why wouldn't you do it whatever it takes?

An intrapreneur is an entrepreneurial spirit within a very large organization. This is someone who thinks, *"well, why can't we?"* and *"let so-and-so do this,"* or *"I'll just do it."*

Our kids are seen as disruptive because they're constantly asking why. They'll say, *"well, why can't you do that?"* and *"who said so?"* and *"what if?"* Then they're told to sit down and shut up. These kids probably have very good reasons to ask why, because they don't accept the status quo, and that's what innovation is all about.

It's seeing a better way of doing it. Some people just shrug their shoulders and think, *"Ok, I'll just accept it,"* and there are others that think, *"well surely we can do this better, faster, with more impact - I'm sure we can."*

AirBnB is a good example. AirBnB was just some guys who wanted somewhere to sleep during conference weekends, so they put a mattress on someone's floor.

Virgin Atlantic is another. Richard Branson was told his flight was cancelled, and he was like, *"surely there must be someone somewhere."* He found a company that could charter a plane for 200 people. He went back to the gate and said, *"listen guys, I can get you a flight out of here for $200 each; who's in?"* And that's how Virgin Atlantic was started.

An entrepreneurial spirit is relentless. It's wired not to accept no. It's often easier sometimes to say no: you've got too much work or it's too much of a pain. But intrinsically, an entrepreneur knows when to say yes, however difficult it feels in terms of logistics, and they'll get it done somehow.

I was now in a very large enterprise, nearly 2,000 people. I needed help to knock down the silos across the group companies and engage the hunters.

We called them the *"Lab Rats"*. No one else had bothered to pay these people any attention. I called them my *"Rough Diamonds."* Nurturing their talents proved to be a crucial component in the long-term success of this entire project.

Every Monday I hosted get-togethers where I would introduce people who might not otherwise have met. Of course, some of the people I brought would spend the whole meeting on their BlackBerry, not even recognizing the networking opportunity.

Those were the people who wouldn't connect with anyone. These are the people who miss out on life. They certainly hardly relate or recognize the value of those around them. They were destined to miss out on the incredible opportunities that were swirling in those rooms. At first I felt sad that they were missing out but that soon went. I know I couldn't save everyone.

Attendees who didn't spend the get-togethers on their phones wound up meeting the people who would come to define their careers. They did it because they had the character and the quality to do so. Many of these people remain close compatriots to this day. Aside from the networking opportunities, I used those Monday morning induction meetings to assure new joiners that there was space for them to innovate. I'd show them around the physical space and then I'd give them a 15-20 minute presentation about what it was we were doing at the Labs. I'd say, *"there'll be some of you that will be really inspired by this and others not so much. And that's fine. But just know that there's a place that if you want to be an intrapreneur, you can."*

It was natural that some of those new joiners would never be heard from again. But others would feel inspired by the vague notion of something different and new. Perhaps just as you were inspired to pick up this book.

They'd shoot me an email or pop by my office, and soon enough they'd be collaborating on projects around the Labs. For me this could be valuable by just acting as a defender of the Labs in other areas of the agency.

I was recruiting the hunters the ones hungry for value. The farmers would remain the ones who would wind up on their deathbed somehow regretting that they didn't do more. The hunter mentality would keep moving forward with wanting to effect change to make it better.

By saying yes - who know where it can lead. In my case I certainly didn't know. I couldn't have imagined I would be judging on the innovation juries for Cannes Lion, Eurobest, D&AD or SXSW

or writing this book!

But that's the point. I didn't know but it didn't stop me. Not knowing drove me and it meant I was unencumbered by any projection or expectation.

Yes, it takes time, but the journey makes you. You get there in the end by staying on the course that's set by your heart and your instinct. It works by not allowing anyone to take you off the road you know feels right - even though everyone sees you're still laying it.

Problem: Technology is changing at a rapid pace.

Solution: Move away from your desk and get curious.

9

THE SIX R'S
MEASURING SUCCESS AS AN INTRAPRENEUR

*A*new way at the time was, to measure success that is more holistic and human than a spreadsheet.

One of the reasons why clients work with agencies is to buy the creativity they don't have full time access to inside their own business. Increasingly this is changing as clients start to make thinking and innovation more what they do and less what they outsource.

We built the Labs to make sure that clients would find even more reasons to come to us. We would be more creative that way. We provided a way to understand the incredible rate and pace of change taking place. It was a way to stay smart. It was a smart way to get smarter. How were we able to show success to management, that wasn't specifically just about the bottom line spreadsheet item.

A big part of being a maverick is being smart. Street smart. Not arrogant. Just knowing enough to stay ahead of trouble. I guess some would say *"hustle"*- but that really is the life of an intrapreneur.

The ability to make something happen from nothing and magic something up just because you can. It's instinct most of the time. I'm not sure that can be learned in school with exams. There's a saying that the best form of defense is offense, but for me it was more about having better answers than anyone else. There's a balance in that too. Nobody likes a smug smart arse.

My approach was always to listen, look, and then provide answers. Sometimes I would come to the party with answers in my mind that could help identify the right question too.

It's questions that drive the creative mind. Every time I went to take a brief, I was always waiting for the moment for the penny to be dropped - for the actual question to emerge.

The Questions:

On Innovation - How do we find the innovators? Do they come ready made? Where is it best to uncover them? How do we give them the right space within which to flourish?

On Talent - The opportunities for talent and the demands of talent have changed hugely in the last ten years. Do we know what employees expect in 2019 and is that different to what they expected in 2009?

On Work - Given all the changes in the world do we now need multiple inputs to make us more fulfilled? Is the idea of only having one job out of date?

On Workspace/Place - Do we need to put the same demands on people as we have for so many years? 9-5, 25 days holiday a year. Surely, we can work differently, remotely, and whenever we want?

On Recruitment - As an employer what do we need to do to attract the right people?

On Organization - How should we organize to work? We see new movements like Holacracy and Teal. Will we see a fundamental shift in how organizations structure and motivate?

These are business challenges, and yet the answers to them are all about creativity and innovation. They require thinking with the disrupter's mind. I actually had to answer questions like these as I set up my own organization - the Labs.

I Described My Problem

How to have a lean, non-hierarchical structure within a global organization that allows me to be an intrapreneur.

Take a look at Ricardo Semler, who took over his father's company, Semco (founded in 1954) at the age of 19. Not only did he turn the company round, he made it an outstanding success. On the brink of bankruptcy in 1980, Semco achieved revenues of

$34 million in 1993 and $160 million in 2000. Semler threw out the rule book: for example, workers make their own decisions; every corporate decision is put to the vote; people turn up to the meetings they want to be at. It sounds insane, but it works.

Together We Developed The 6 'R's Of Innovation

We knew that we needed a framework to make sure that we had an answer to the question about value, and we knew that we would need to measure our value on criteria that would go way beyond revenue or profit. The management behind large corporations only ever seem to measure in one unit - that of the incoming dollars on a spreadsheet. Initially this whole idea was brainstormed with Giles Rhys Jones and Olivia Rzepczynski in the early days of Labs being formed.

The Labs needed to come up with alternative measures of success. We needed something that would be just enough to show we were bringing other forms of value. By today's standards of value these will seem simplistic, but this was a major leap for the agency. Remember, we were seen as a cost center - although we were just initially two people on salary (myself and Joanne Bloom) and to be spread thinly across a group of 1800 people, 10 group marketing communication companies.

We had to show value and constantly question how much we were really valued. Innovation has long been a popular buzzword within business, and for good reason. To me, innovation was never just about bringing money in, it was about creating value for clients and our creative teams. It was therefore also about bring about a revolution in our way of working.

We decided to measure our work by what we called the 6 'R's of innovation success:

1. *Revenue*
2. *Reputation*
3. *Recruitment*
4. *Retention*
5. *Relationships*
6. *Responsibility*

It was a simple enough device to remember and had the right effect inside the agency.

Revenue

We knew we would need to have this at the top of our calculation. We also knew that a lot of the work we did and the things we achieved were very difficult to measure in numerical terms. Revenue, however is an easy one to measure, if it is direct. But because everything we did also generated indirect revenue, it wasn't always so straightforward.

The Lab was self-funded, so, everything we did, whether speaking at an event in Dubai, or attending a tech conference in Amsterdam, had to be useful in some way. We had to show results. As a result, we did things the way an entrepreneur would. We applied ingenuity to everything if we talked at a conference, we might get a free ticket to the event, while flying EasyJet and using Airbnb accommodation.

We were really the connectors, there to extend Ogilvy's capability as an agency.

Reputation

Amongst all this change, we had a great opportunity to stand out. To drive the change and be a pathfinder. To build a reputation out of all the complexity.

Although Labs was way ahead of its time, enough people could see the sense of that. They just didn't know how to make it happen. Ogilvy is extremely well-known in the advertising and marketing world. It's a global-scale agency. It has formidable size and reputation in its industry, but outside of that nobody really knows much about it. Ogilvy needed to be expert in every industry because its clients were in every industry. We couldn't only know advertising really well.

Through the Labs we would spend a lot of time in every industry sector raising the overall profile of what Ogilvy does. This would excite new clients, and we would learn new stuff from them. For example, we would sponsor 3D print shows, our name would be attached and the suppliers would think of us if they ever needed an advertising agency.

We would do workshops, talks, gather contacts, and increase our visibility and earn a reputation way outside the advertising sphere. We would pursue really random things that we just found interesting to make sure that we're really plugged into other areas.

Recruitment

Finding talent is always a challenge for agencies, especially the biggest ones who had plenty of competition for the big-name agencies. We had the Rough Diamond program - the collaboration between disrupters and innovators in educational learning. We partnered with these educational organizations to identify, develop, and nurture new creative talent. The whole point was to try and diversify our recruitment and our business as a whole.

We partnered with an organization called The Ideas Foundation. It was all about getting the more unruly kids into the creative industry by showing them how they could be creative and interested in developing a career for themselves.

We would identify the disrupters. They were on the edge of disaster in a traditional sense. We wanted those kids who were really wanting to work with creativity. We either funded their education at the School of Communication Arts, an advertising-specific college in London or they would enroll at a university called Ravensbourne in Greenwich.

We won the National Undergraduate Employability Award for the best collaboration with a university. As an industry we needed to diversify and build much more ethnicity. We were probably one of the pathfinder industries in terms of lesbian, gay, bisexual, and transgender equality.

Retention

Keeping the best people when we had discovered them. People were coming and going all the time. It's a perennial problem. Keeping the best people was what drove me.

That meant giving our people reasons to stay and be involved with the agency. For us it was about creating a place within the agency that allowed people to do different things - things that would actually inspire them.

If you were getting a bit bored with your day job or you wanted something to add on, you could do something different, through the Labs. We only had three employees, so extra resources to do different kinds of projects were always welcome.

The Lab produced six-month research projects - The Semesters of Learning that ended with a conference called Lab Day. We looked for people around the agency who wanted to volunteer to help bring that event together.

Relationships

It seems obvious to us these days that new networks and new connections is what makes the world go around. Back then it was always viewed by narrowed eyes. It was like we were planning to give the crown jewels away. But we knew it was the opposite and we all stood to gain by getting out there and encouraging new shoots. I have always believed that from small acorns grow big trees. We don't know what it looks like straight away, but in time and with patience it grows in all manner of directions that can surprise and delight. This is all about a long-term strategy, not a quick win on a financial spreadsheet.

There were two official relationships for Ogilvy Labs - the Knowledge Transfer Network, which was part of the government's Innovate UK network, and Collider, an accelerator dedicated to marketing and advertising startups. This helped brands and agencies identify, understand, engage with, and sell to their consumers. But in terms of partnerships, nothing written down - but on a handshake and no money changing hands just paying forward and sharing. The partnerships were the black book of which there were literally thousands.

We invested real capital in these startups; we coached them through a highly structured program, and we connected them to potential corporate customers and investors.

It is important that businesses build an awareness of startups. We worked with a lot already and we made sure that we were always finding the new ones out there, trying to tease out more and more interesting examples. Many of the case studies you will see in the book are with startups. They were the brave ones experimenting with the Lab. No one else was doing this in such a structured way as we were. The semesters of learning would have been charged out by a McKinsey or consultants for millions. It's super smart thinking that Ogilvy got free of charge. Not just the thinking, but the implementation each and every six months. It would seem the outside world found it to be more exciting than inside the organization, because the day job was still the way to pay salaries.

There always had to be a mutual benefit though. It was not a case of finding a startup and asking, *"what can you provide to Ogilvy and our clients?"*, it was always about what Ogilvy and our clients can provide to the startup.

These relationships matter because you need to recognize that you and your business cannot know everything. Knowing and understanding other innovators will help you build a better business.

Responsibility

Even then I was always passionate about giving back to those less privileged or just to be accountable and think about the world around us. As a company Ogilvy had a corporate social responsibility strategy and so we pushed that idea hard in the Labs. We were very focused on giving something back. We did a lot of work in the community such as mentoring at schools.

We were always looking to inspire people through technology. We would be running classes to get girls into coding and HTML. There would be a lot of pro bono work with charities helping them fundraise. This is where I met with Kerry, her case study and story will be featured later. Dave Birss and Ruth came up with the Ideas Shop, a way for Ogilvy to give ideas away for free for the local communities. It was a genius way to give back. Kerry was one of the beneficiaries of my mentorship time at one of the ideas shops. Little did either of us know of the exciting times ahead that would extend many, many years in to the future.

We conducted our work with the 6 'R's of Innovation in mind at all times. They acted as our yardstick, our defense mechanism and the baseline measurement for everything we did. While not every one of the six measures of success needed to be present in all cases, nor exhaustive we would always apply them as a test to everything we ever did.

Getting away from the bottom line is always valuable. We developed an open-minded, conscientious, and thoughtful approach to our business. As a result, we became a much more appealing business to work with, to work for, and it kept us in an agile position as the world continued to change around us.

Working In A Whole World Of Change

When you talk about people who innovate, you are talking about the people who like change. These people are willing to try something new. In fact, they seek it out. They are on the front foot of change - not just *"being changed."*

When change is all around and happening to you, you can't just say, *"no, I'm not doing that."* You don't have a say in how things change, but you do have a say in how you react to it.

Intrapreneurs and entrepreneurs have all their fingers and toes on the pulse of change. We have to position ourselves in front of the next wave and prepare to get swept up by it. Standing on the shore and watching it will never work.

> Intrapreneurs and entrepreneurs have all their fingers and toes on the pulse of change. We have to position ourselves in front of the next wave and prepare to get swept up by it. Standing on the shore and watching it will never work.

Change is relentless. In the financial industry, it's said that by the time you read it in the Wall Street Journal, there's no deal left. If you're getting your news from the newspapers, you're behind the curve. To really be at the forefront of change, as an intrapreneur needs to be, you have to build your own and then rely on a system of peer-to-peer knowledge. When the pilot Sully safely landed an Airbus 320 in the Hudson those of us on Twitter found out before the news channels and journalists. Times continuously bring change.

Twitter is ahead of the news. There's many blogs and channels to get your fix of what's going on around you. You don't have to rely on Rupert Murdoch anymore. You can see a trend across many industries. They're all being disrupted and transformed beyond recognition.

Think about any industry you want. Take the auto industry and peer-to-peer models like Uber. Whatever you may think of them now, they had a very disruptive idea and they carried it out.

In the 50's you would own your own car, in the 70's it was all about renting with Avis and Hertz, and now you've got Whipcar, where you leave your car outside your house and a stranger can drive it around for the day when you're not using it. Technology has been a major agent for change and its hugely influencing social change. It's become more than a sharing economy; it's now a fluid and fractured economy.

I read something recently by a blogger from Chicago, Zander Nethercutt who sums up the world today and especially just how much the game has changed.

"Now, in a world in which information is becoming less and less imperfect all the time, and the costs of advertising are ever decreasing per the increased word of mouth facilitated by avenues like YouTube and Facebook, the advantage enjoyed by large companies is fast dissipating.

Dollar Shave Club's success indicates that the prevalence of shotgun advertising will fade over the decades to come. Companies that serve the masses will be replaced by companies that serve niches, because the latter will take advantage of the vastly decreased distribution costs and effective avenues for grassroots marketing that the internet provides. As this happens, and information about both buyers and suppliers become more and more perfect, the advantages enjoyed by producers of homogenous products like the Big Mac and Coke will dissipate, and their products will lose market share to more targeted, higher quality products that take advantage of unique, niche markets that were never able to be recognized, or more correctly, monetized, in the old world of advertising. The internet, the data it generates, and the companies that own and utilize that data best, will be the driving forces behind the monetization of niches."

There are many examples, but there are too few intrapreneurs. Large organizations need intrapreneurs to see all these changes happening and help them decide what to do. It will never be any single person's responsibility to see these changes happening. It's too enormous a data set. Nowadays these calculations are so complex that we have to rely on algorithms, robotics and machines that learn to help us calculate what's going on and decide what to do next.

People running the business don't necessarily have the wherewithal to have their finger on the pulse of what's coming in their own industry. You need someone to be the spotter, to look outside and connect.

The intrapreneur takes a long-termview. It requires a perspective and that is hard for some people. Some may discount it as superfluous because it can sometimes take years to see the results of these kinds of experiments.

We were careful never to make people feel daft, but there were many occasions when we were probably a bit too far ahead of the curve. It just drove us to communicate harder. Sometimes, it's just about timing. The right time, the right place and then it hits a tipping point. Then finally people get it. Sometimes, it's difficult to think *"well, I talked about this ten years ago"*, but it just wasn't ready to hit mainstream. It's ready when it's ready and enough of us are pushing it through. Being ahead of the curve means that when it does hit, that we are the ones that know. We have been eating, sleeping, breathing this world, it's our job. As I mentioned previously, the good people know the good people. That's how we work.

A large business is rather like an oil tanker, it can't turn on a dime. Smaller, agile startups have an easier time adjusting to technological or social changes, but these large companies have ossified legacy systems and long-standing processes.

Not surprisingly, it's why the large companies end up partnering or learning (often too late) from the little startups as they are so much more nimble. The large organizations may have the desire to change, and they need people within their own organization who can reach out and help that happen.

A good intrapreneur knows that there's always a way. You might get ten no's, but the eleventh ask might be a yes, and that's all you need. At times don't even ask to get a NO, just do it because once that *"no"* comes out of someone's mouth, then it is harder to make it happen. So, most of the time we would go under the radar and come back up when it was finished. Sorry. Too late. It's been done! That shows guts and determination. There are no guidelines. Remember, if it was easy, then everyone would be doing it!

A good intrapreneur knows when she's taken on too much, and she knows exactly who to call to get some help with that.

A good intrapreneur can read people. People used to think Dave Trott was a bad boss, but I knew better. He was strict for sure, but no one else noticed that when he had his dark glasses on, it meant that he couldn't get his contact lenses in. He was tired and a little cranky, so it probably wasn't a good time to get help with something. A good intrapreneur pays attention.

The concept of the 6 'R's was fundamental to our understanding of intrapreneurship. During this time, it was a really useful tool for everyone to work within. It was almost a template for innovation. Over and over again throughout my career, it's proven a simple way to test for trends that haven't yet gone mainstream. I know it's not an exhaustive set of measures for everything, but it proved time and again to be simple enough to defend great work against the attack of the purely finance driven mind.

I used the 6 'R's to put a measure of success to the semesters. So, we can talk about revenue. That's when a client will pay for, say, the IBM Wimbledon 3D printing Job or Rory's talks, or any of those kinds of tangible revenues that got paid into Ogilvy's account.

The 6 'R's: A Reputation Case Study

For every project, we would always do a film. This meant we had something tangible that could be entered into awards to showcase what you've done. One example is the Power of Cute, the film that came out of the behavioral change semester.

We were working on launching Ogilvy Change, a sector of the agency focused on behavioural economics. We were going to launch their website, but wanted something tangible to go with it. Some Ogilvy creatives, myself and a planner called Tara came up with this idea of painting babies on shutters. We got the permissions, and we were ready to start painting, and the shopkeeper said, *"I'm not having a white baby on my shutter."* That was the day we were due to do all the graffiti. But anyway, to cut a long story short, we made it happen. We filmed it. And over the course of six months, the babies weren't vandalized, because the babies' faces were making people calm. You don't need all these policemen on the street: you can just use behavioral cues to get people to behave well.

We showed behavioral concepts in a practical way, and we had a film that we could use as a measure of our success. It would be something tangible we could use to launch Ogilvy Change.

We asked the Creative Director three or four times to do the film, because I had run out of money within the Lab, and they normally would put these films together out of their budget. He would not have it. I went above his head, and his boss said to ask a different CD, and we found a crazy director who would do it. Lo and behold, the film won a Gold Cannes Lion.

I saw that first director on the Carlton Terrace in Cannes shortly thereafter. He tried to walk past me, but obviously I wasn't going to let him.

There was this moment where he kind of came up and said, *"Congratulations,"* with an obvious feeling of awkwardness, and there was a moment where I'm looking in his eyes and he's looking in my eyes, and he knew that I knew that he made a mistake. That's all I needed to do. That's all that someone that's disruptive, needs to do. They don't need to be given rewards of god-knows-how much money; that, for that kind of disruptive personality, is reward enough, is getting the job done, is showing it to be incredibly successful.

Now, what happens is large corporates reinvent the story. You have to be sure to tell your side of the story, even if it sounds like you're blowing your own trumpet. If you don't, the truth will be invented by other people to get the credit.

> You have to be sure to tell your side of the story, even if it sounds like you're blowing your own trumpet, because if you don't, the truth will be invented by other people to get the credit.

Tara Austin explains this story so eloquently in her own words to add color to this particular project.

Babies of the Borough - Gold Cannes Lion Awarded Case Study:

Once upon a time, I was the Head Girl of my school. As you can probably imagine this means I am pretty good at playing by the rules. I'd never thought of myself as difficult or a disruptor or even someone who particularly enjoys change, but that was until I joined Ogilvy and met Nicole Yershon.

Nicole helped me realize that in the marketing industry, while you can certainly "get ahead" by playing by the rules and following the formula, looking "professional" and using the jargon, ultimately that path takes you towards money, power and exhaustion - not the thing that I actually wanted, which was to help get my creative ideas made.

They say that people won't remember what you say, only how you make them feel. Well I can't remember when I first met Nicole, but I can certainly remember how she treated me. From day one, when I was only a "Junior Planner" she insisted on referring to me in conversation as a "Senior Planner" and when I tried to correct this she further insisted I was twice the strategist of most of those she knew. She always talked me up. Being very "English" about these things (and without her Jewish chutzpah) it used to embarrass me when she'd tell people how clever and creative I was as I was standing in front of them. I used to refer to her as "my PR machine" but the fact is that from the very beginning she saw something in me that perhaps even I didn't know was there.

It all began with music. With a family background in the record industry I have always been passionate about music in communications and with Nicole and a few others together we decided to run one of her infamous "Lab Days" focused on the power of audio. But we didn't stop at the usual conference of speakers and exhibitors. For some reason we decided it would be a good idea to hold a day-long music festival in our own office complete with three stages of live music concurrently streamed to our clients and offices worldwide. Nine months of planning went into executing "Lab Day Live" and the stresses and strains and number of people who told us we couldn't do it bonded Nicole and I forever.

That was just the beginning.

It was the week after the London riots and the editorial recalled that day when our city seemed to be self-destructing. Normality had resumed a week on, but the questions still clung. What would possess people to destroy their own neighborhoods and loot the little, local businesses that served them? How could people burn down the pub that they drank in and loot the shop where they bought their paper? These were places that served them. These were places that were run by local people like them. The rioters weren't rioting in Mayfair, they were rioting in their own communities. Unless we understood it how could we stop it from happening again? Enlightenment came in the most unlikely place - the Grocer magazine.

Angered by what had happened to his readership during the riots, the Editor asked the government to relax the planning laws on installing shop security shutters. Insight emerged into the planning process, revealing the battle shopkeepers had to enter into to install them and why town planners hated them so vehemently.

In the ivory towers of Canary Wharf, this article made me reflect on something I'd never had cause to consider before: shop shutters. These seemingly insignificant devices line the high streets of every town in our country – even the smallest of corner-shops in the smallest of hamlets, pulls down their shutters at night. Yet despite being everywhere, I'd never truly noticed them before.

The "broken windows theory" made famous in the 1990's by NYC Police Commissioner Bill Bratton, suggests that small environmental cues can have a catalytic effect on crime and antisocial behavior. One broken window quickly leads to two - through the unconscious assumption that, since no one repairs a single window, the area is effectively lawless. Two broken windows lead to a break in. And so on...

Shutters are a similar cue. They don't just "bring down the area"; subconsciously they bring down our collective psyche. By treating us all like anonymous criminals, they alienate us from the people that live and work behind their steel walls saying: "this is not a place to linger, this is not a place to belong." By signaling the lawlessness of the area, and masking the community behind the shutters, they are a provocation rather than just protection. Perhaps the shutters, and all that they symbolize, were a part of the reason the riots happened in the first place.

Yet, the Grocer was right; shopkeepers want and need shutters. After all, they're only really conscious of them at the end of a long night keeping their shop safe. That's exactly why they are totally ubiquitous – the steel fortresses are there to serve a blunt purpose. They're not going to go away. So, what could be done?

An answer could be found in the "good" shutters. I thought of the pretty, pastel images that adorn shutters on the seafront in my hometown of Hastings. These shutters were considered to be "street art", not street furniture. After all, aren't shutters large, relatively flat surfaces, ripe to carry an image? Surely a shutter could be utilized as a media space, one that could carry a message like any conventional Out of Home? If so, could they even carry a message so positive that it inverted everything the shutters currently stood for? Instead of providing a bare physical barrier to entry, perhaps shutters could carry a message that made them a more powerful, moral barrier.

What message could do this? Inquiring within the Ogilvy behavioral sciences fraternity one clear opportunity arose. What better way to humanize something intimidatingly inhuman, than by literally giving it a human face – and better still, the face of an innocent, the face of a baby. This was more than a hunch. In the 1940's ethologist Konrad Lorenz first proposed the "baby schema," as a set of infantile features – the large head, round face and big eyes so beloved by Disney – which motivates care-taking behavior. More recently, in 2009, Melanie Glocker and a team at the Universities of Muenster and Pennsylvania provided the first experimental proof of this evolutionary effect. It had been proven that "cute" matters to the brain. For hidden within "cute" were the cues of helplessness that make us aware of our responsibility to nurture.

Consider, for a moment, how much of our sleeping-kitten-laughing-baby-YouTube-browsing behavior the baby schema answers. For we actively enjoy the effect "cute" has by reminding us these small creatures are dependent upon our actions; it softens and re-focuses our minds, investing us with an importance. To a defenseless little baby, we know we are everything that matters.

A simple idea emerged: to find somewhere that had been badly affected by the riots and paint the faces of local babies onto the security shutters - to help encourage people to see their community as a living, breathing entity, of which they are a part. In reversing the negativity of the shutters using the babies' faces, we would undertake an experiment in social cohesion. Could we actually reduce antisocial behavior in the area, with something as simple as a lick of paint?

This was where Nicole came in.

Because an idea is only as good as those who actually make it happen and Nicole is someone who "does."

She loved the idea. She wanted to make it happen and not only that, she had her own private "pot" to fund it and all the right connections to find the right place to do it. Woolwich, within the Borough of Greenwich, was badly affected by the riots and Nicole had links to the Council. It was here that we would run our experiment.

Between us we enlisted a small crack team to work secretly, using a weekly status meeting over nine months to plan the experiment. To use Nicole's very favorite phrase, we worked "under the radar" to get it done without the perfectionism and people saying no that would hold us back. It didn't need to be perfect, it needed to "be." Nicole showed me that working in beta was the only way to get anything done. There were hundreds of set-backs and doing everything alongside the day-job proved impossible at times. But we persisted. We followed the idea, and even when we couldn't execute things the way we wanted to we found new ways. That's just her spirit. With Nicole a problem is simply a challenge to be overcome or maneuvered around.

Dealing with the local council was what can only, euphemistically, be termed "an experience." At one moment they over-enthusiastically wanted to invest tax-payers money into our scheme, the next they dogmatically sought to stop us from launching our campaign on the first anniversary of the riots or "disturbances" as they insisted on calling them (one life lesson of the experience was that when people refuse to use plain English, there's usually something badly wrong).

What seemed like a small endeavor to paint a parade of shops quickly became a logistical nightmare of dealings with the council, getting permission from non-contactable, non-English-speaking shopkeepers and working around shop opening-times on long summer nights, not to mention recruiting the all-important babies. After one particular set-back with the Council where they had changed their mind yet again about giving us access to a number of shops and shutters, Nicole and I simply took to the streets ourselves petitioning every shopkeeper individually. I'll never forget us brazenly walking into the male-dominated betting shops of Woolwich asking to see the owners about their shutters. It was uncomfortable. It wasn't easy. But that was the point. She taught me that the worst that could happen was that you made something happen.

And we did. Having made some serious compromises thanks to council red tape and having to enlist and pay for outside help to manage the logistics of painting the shutters, we somehow completed the project in time for the first anniversary of the riots and in doing so, quite to our astonishment, generated millions of media impressions worldwide. But it was the idea, rather than the small execution, which captured imaginations. For the coverage showed us that although the London riots had happened right here to us, what we were doing had a global relevance. It helped us realize that from Rio to Rotterdam shutters are a global, if unspoken, scourge on society, signaling the same negative associations the world over – and that babies too have a fascinatingly equal and opposite, universal power over the human mind.

It was an idea that was even worth a Gold Lion in Cannes. Again, Nicole was the champion here. For while I saw the "Babies of the Borough" as something I wanted us to try, I had never considered the potential for it to be recognized. The first creative director at our agency didn't want to enter it for the Awards in Cannes. He didn't think it was good enough or big enough, but Nicole, along with the creative team involved, wouldn't take no for an answer and took the idea to another creative director team who instantly saw the potential.

Five years on from that experience and with help from the MET police we have seen that our experiment worked. It reduced anti-social behavior in the area of the Babies by ten percent versus a control and we are due to shortly roll out another "Babies of the Borough" experiment in West Ealing as part of Ogilvy's Behavioral Interventions agency, Ogilvy Change for which I am now the Creative Strategy Director. None of this would have been possible without the woman who funded and forced through Ogilvy Change's inaugural experiment and who made me the woman I am today - no longer the Head Girl, no longer unhappy to rock the boat. I know now that if you want to do something creative it won't be easy, there will be many people happy to doubt and criticize your idea, there will be set-backs, conflict and inevitable politics. People are jealous and people don't like change. They find people like Nicole threatening and difficult because they only know a good thing when they see it and Nicole sees a good thing before it is a good thing. She sees potential for things that others find uncomfortable, just like she saw the potential in me that made me feel so awkward at the time.

Have there been times I have got into trouble because of Nicole Yershon? Yes. Have there been times I have ever regretted that trouble. No. As long as I keep on learning.

The Silicon Roundabout Tour

The measures the 6 'R's gave us the framework. We developed the 6 'R's as a metric by which to quantify the success of each Semester of Learning and to push pack against the single measure of revenue. That way we could go somewhere like Silicon Roundabout - a small corner of London dedicated to leading edge technology, creativity and startups.

I had a goal in mind. I could come out of it knowing that I had connected two people who would go on to do something amazing, even if I couldn't imagine it at the time.

It would have been really easy to go to all these events, NOT talk to anybody and consider it a success, but I had the 6 'R's to keep me accountable. It meant something important to me.

During the Silicon Roundabout tour, the result was Rory's book. I couldn't have known when I went that I would have come away with that as a specific outcome, but there was an outcome.

So now I had a wonderful way of raising more funds for the Lab R&D pot, with Rory's book - by offering not only Rory to speak at events as his agent, but also as his publisher, offer his book at publisher costs. Finding other ways to find revenue isn't easy. There is never an easy way.

Like I've said the 6 'R's are not an exhaustive set of measures. They were what we all needed at the time to defend ourselves against a big and brutal enterprise heavily biased towards revenue and profit at all costs.

Problem: Not being able to measure success.

Solution: The 6 'R's of Innovation: Revenue, Reputation, Retention of existing staff, Recruiting diverse talent, Relationships (The Black Book), and Responsibility (giving back).

10

THE BLACK BOOK - IT'S ALL ABOUT PEOPLE

*7*he secret weapon of this intrapreneur became the little black book. For me it's where the magic begins.

There's a very famous definition of insanity.

It relates perfectly to how some businesses seem to think. They think that by doing the same thing in the same way over and over again they can expect a result that still works in an entirely different world.

They seem to think that everything can stay the same as the world becomes completely unrecognizable in the way it functions. They cling to the predictable, everything in line with quarterly reporting to shareholders, money still coming in as it always used to mentality.

Their vision describes a world so entirely opposite to mine. Disruption, however you choose to define it, is happening daily and globally. It affects everything from business, politics, large and small organizations and individuals. Our lives are completely at the mercy of a technological revolution. Technology is firmly integrated into everyone and everything. Any business not looking at how digital technology is going to affect every system and process; business model and operating behavior is going to fail.

My challenge was to try and save as many souls from drowning as humanly possible.

It seems trite to say it, but people are everything.

The advertising industry is a people business but one that's still beset by old fashioned processes and systems. For me to survive those years, it was important to add more human values, emotional intelligence, and human connection. The sum of all of that became The Little Black Book.

In my experience, there's nothing quite like doing business by the whites of your eyes. Innovating is scary. Being outside of your comfort zone is scary. By its very nature, absolutely terrifying. You have to trust your coworkers. And you have to trust yourself.

Even how this book came about, was to do with my connection with people. I was on a boat. It was invitation only - The Summit at Sea. The event was for 3,000 people from all around the globe. It gathered a group of the brightest people in business and culture for a voyage in international waters.

Summit is designed to do one thing exceptionally well - forcing innovative, interesting people to get off their phones get them to meet new people, face to face with no distractions.

When I met Jesse, the publisher of this book, there were no business cards exchanged, because we were sitting in a Jacuzzi talking to each other as human beings.

It was only after we left the boat that I could seek him out and reconnect online. We were able to have good honest chats about who we were, not about what we did for a living. That came later in the conversation.

It led to Jesse telling me that I had a *"book inside me"*- this book. He thought I had a great story to tell. You only get these types of conversations in environments that are away from your desk and certainly not in typical meetings.

The interesting stuff always seems to happen in between and out of our comfort zone. The previous year, did I know I was going to be made redundant or that I was going to publish a book, NO! I had no idea. That is the beauty of saying *"yes"* borne from human interactions and conversations.

The sum total of all these interactions, conversations and connections comprise my black book.

I don't mean to sound like a doe-eyed naive 22-year-old by saying, *"I'm going to take on the world"* but in a lot of ways that's what it was like to me. A tiny team of good people set against a massive behemoth of an enterprise - populated by people who were used to working in a particular way and within strict rules.

A focus only on profitability and margin.

I attack disruption with a more sober approach, one that I've gained from decades of hard work at the bleeding edge of corporate innovation. And I used to be that doe-eyed 22-year-old, bulldozing my way through corporate red tape. It took the loss of my mother and the end of my marriage to teach me the art of more empathetic disruption.

Success in business has less to do with intellectual intelligence and far more with emotional intelligence (EI). In the Lab teams, I regularly had everyone undertake emotional intelligence testing.

I discovered that our team had complementary strengths: where I struggled, Gemma excelled, and vice versa. In the early days of our intelligence testing, I always scored the lowest on empathy. I had to learn the hard way. It wasn't that I didn't care, I just hadn't experienced despair or major challenges to know what it felt like for others.

> You have to understand what the lesson is and take responsibility for your own actions. If you don't then you never really learn to understand yourself.

I was sad if they were sad, but actually *feeling* what they felt, the empathy, well that was something that only the journey of life teaches you. Life is a hard teacher and you have to really pay attention. You have to understand what the lesson is and take responsibility for your own actions. If you don't then you never really learn to understand yourself.

To this day, it still makes me wonder how many corporate leaders have the appropriate emotional intelligence to deal with the new world in which they need to operate. It's a fact that our IQ doesn't change that much. It's a combination of nature and nurture - partly your essential nature and partly the schooling you receive.

Jim Collins explains this well. He states that *"boards of Directors typically believe that transforming a company from good to great requires an extreme personality, an egocentric chief to lead the corporate charge."*

He says the essential ingredient for taking a company to greatness is having a Level 5 leader. This translates as *"an executive in whom extreme personal humility blends paradoxically with intense professional will."* He identifies the characteristics common to Level

5 leaders as follows - *"humility, iron will, ferocious resolve, and the tendency to give credit to others while assigning blame to themselves."*

Emotional Intelligence though, is constantly in flux. It's a function of the adversity you face and how you respond to it. My own adversity has resulted in tremendous emotional benefits. Some would look at my challenging few years and ask how I could possibly have coped. But we all do. And I lived through it and living through it allowed me to hone my capacity for empathy and for belief in myself. It was a function of attitude and belief that I could learn my way through it.

Most people try to keep things flat. They want stability.

They want the comfort of a nine to five job, day after day, year after year. But that's no way to grow. Living the full spectrum of highs and lows, risks and rewards and losses works far better. It has made me who I am.

The ups and downs are like a heartbeat - if it is flat, then that would mean you are dead - a flat line. I didn't ever live my life like that. I came to learn that with great highs come great lows and that is the beauty of life.

I've always understood that people do things because they want to. Not because you're telling them to. Not because it's the right thing to do logically. They do it for their own reasons, because they like you or they like the project they are working on. They are motivated one way or another.

Respect, I learnt, is how you get shit done. Don't micromanage people. However old they are, everyone has their own unique way of doing things and that means they are always bringing new learning to the party.

It is crucial to be open hearted and, most of all, open minded. There isn't just one way to do something. I have learnt most from others. I find it is really important to relax and welcome in others. They will bring a new way of doing things and most of the time it will be a revelation for you. It was for me - especially with the Rough Diamonds over the years (See Chapter 12).

I contrasted my Black Book with the Yellow Pages.

The Yellow Pages, as we know, is simply a list of names and numbers. Perfectly useful if you know all the people and know you want them, but nothing compared to my Black Book. My Black Book is beyond a list. It's people that I have vetted and probably worked with and now love and trust.

I know their passions, their hobbies, their goals. I know that even if we haven't spoken in a few years, I could call them up and get right to work. Trust and respect go a long way, they are actually how you really get shit done. Not by saying jump and expecting someone to say how high. That is not the way it works anymore - it's all people power now and the fact that everyone is their own brand. The people in my Black Book are people I've nurtured over time, not expecting immediate returns but knowing that I was building authentic, trusting relationships. It's really all about treating people ow they want to be treated.

Forget about business; everyone, every waiter, every busboy, every Financial Director in the world is the protagonist of their own biography and therefore worthy of respect.

When you see every single person as beautiful and worthy of dignity, you're able to give to them because you can. You offer them opportunities; you connect them with other people in their line of work. You don't do it for your career, but it helps, because every time you do someone a favor you end up building up your registry and record of people. I call it paying forward, just because you can. Plus the fact it uses up way less energy to be nice is a bonus. People you can call on when the shit hits the fan. A good leader or a good intrapreneur is someone who is constantly training and retraining her mind. Intrapreneurs are always flexing the muscle of testing and learning. The intrapreneur

> Forget about business; everyone, every waiter, every busboy, every Financial Director in the world is the protagonist of their own biography and therefore worthy of respect.

is always thinking, always testing and always making decisions and moving forward. Top leadership qualities are humility and an iron will.

Intrapreneurs are obsessive connectors. They pick up on the nuances of the worlds they find themselves in at that moment and do what's needed. They do this fast and intuitively. They don't overthink their actions. If you're decent and kind to people and you build relationships, things will probably happen for them and things will probably happen for you.

There's a lot of literature out there right now about how computers are going to put people out of work. There are two ways to look at that. One is to be negative about it and say, *"Oh, shit, the computers are taking over"* - check out *Humans Need Not Apply* on YouTube and resist that change.

But the other way is to be optimistic and say, *"this is great! Computers can do all the dull work, and we can really get to work creating new things."* A true entrepreneur doesn't take change lying down. Digitization obviates human function but also opens up unforeseen opportunities. Digitization also requires new skills. Some jobs will cease to exist, and there will be new jobs.

Eight years ago, between Joanne Bloom and I, we created a role called Creative Lab Technologist for Will Harvey. He started as my first Rough Diamond from Ravensbourne College, and now there are tons of Creative Technologists. That guy became the Head of Innovation at a London ad agency called VCCP and is now Digital Innovation Manager at Diageo.

But here's the anecdote, when we hired him, he occasionally sent round emails with a few typos, especially because of spell check, and people would say to me, *"do you read his emails? That's disgraceful!"* So, I asked him to change the bottom of his emails to say, *"Sorry about the typos; I'm dyslexic."* From then on it was fine - people stopped thinking ill of the person and started to open their minds and hearts towards him.

It's possible to change people's expectations about what's acceptable and what's not. Or that how it used to be done, is not how it is done now. We don't have the formality of letters and then post them, then they arrive two days later. We live in an instant world, an immediately accessible on the go world.

In our lifetimes, things have gone from analog to digital and digital has advanced so rapidly that many people are confused. Others use the change to their advantage. Innovation is all about change and the intrapreneurs are the ones that see the change coming. It just goes to show that when you talk about people who innovate, they're the people who are willing to try something new. It's important to understand that there are a whole lot of other things going on in the organization besides you trying to affect change. From the executives' perspective, you're the thorn in their side saying, *"If you don't do this, you're finished."* They're feeling is, *"I've got to pay all these people's salaries, I've just moved into this massive building and have an enormous rent over our heads, and I can't be listening to this bullshit from this person because I've got proper business to sort out/way bigger things to sort out than listening to her rubbish."*

Because executives are so resistant to change, the intrapreneur must present their ideas strategically and build internal support in order to implement change.

My innate tendency is just to be a tank and go straight to where I need to go. Some people are more naturally political than others. I always listen and feel they want to go where they need to go. But it's likely that I will want to go a different path to them because that will be a more innovative one. I can't help myself. They say black, I will naturally say white, not to be difficult, but to challenge the often lazy status quo. And also, because I will feel there must be a better way. An initially more painful way, but eventually better.

There is certainly a value in knowing how to work with the political. But I would argue that because the pace of change is so quick these days, there's no value in going around upsetting people. You just have to strike a balance between directness and being political.

One method is to get a certain amount of creative license to try something new, and then present it to the executives and say, *"see? Look what we can do at a larger scale!"* Sometimes you have to work under the radar, experiment down there, and then come up to the surface with your results.

The most critical personality traits for an intrapreneur are high emotional intelligence and strong leadership skills. Intrapreneurs need to know they're on the right track without anyone affirming that for them. They're fearless, they have a thirst for knowledge, and they have to be comfortable putting themselves in uncomfortable situations. They are mavericks, twist and turn in all manner of directions, naturally listening and most of all trusting their intuition. On a team, everyone has a role to play. I made every person on my team take the Myers Briggs test. If the personality types are different chess pieces, you're going to need a full set to play effectively. Everyone has their own strengths, and a true leader knows how to play to her employees' strengths rather than castigating them for their weaknesses.

Forbes comes out with the Top 600 Under 30 every so often. I always think that none of these people want to work for a corporate. It's probably because that reminds me of Simon Sinek's talk about how millennials work (if you haven't seen this, it is a must watch!)

In my Semesters of Learning, I noticed that when there was a really bad recession, particularly in Southern Europe, you'd see accelerators and incubators popping up all over the place.

It was because 18 to 24 year-olds couldn't get jobs, but also because there's almost always a lot more opportunity outside of corporate culture. They didn't need the degrees, and they didn't need permission they just made stuff. That's how we got the Internet of Things and the Raspberry Pi and the Arduinos. I saw it in Israel, Portugal, Moscow, Italy, Venice, and Barcelona.

Technology and creativity just responds to what it feels and sees. Just this week, someone tweeted at Elon Musk that they hated queuing for the battery and within six days he'd responded to that tweet and got his whole workforce doing something to create a new product. He's working in a new, entrepreneurial way and it allows him to respond more nimbly to what's happening around him. He naturally and constantly disrupts himself and his company. Most others wouldn't even think of doing that.

I can't remember the name of the Incubator in Athens, but in Italy there was H-Farm. In Russia there was one called Skolkovo, which is interesting because the Russian government has now invested money into building entrepreneurship for the future, not putting them into industry for the first time.

In Portugal, there's something called Beta-I. In Israel there are many. In London there are also many. Gerard Grech, the CEO of Tech City, actually has a presentation of the ecosystem of incubators and accelerators and who's doing what in Europe and the UK.

Silicon Valley isn't the only place where innovation happens.

In corporate culture, when it comes to slashing budgets, the first things to go are the things that don't always produce tangible rewards - incubators, R&D and the think tanks. It's the trips to South by Southwest that can cause alarm to the factory ship businesses because corporate culture just doesn't understand how creativity works.

Part of my approach to work is to spot creativity wherever it is. Often, they are startups and I mentor them. To me they don't disappear. It's about having them in my mind's eye and my finger on the pulse of them all the time.

You put in the hard work, create a meaningful relationship, deliver something of value, and they don't forget you.

During my semesters, I would help them commercialize their product in whatever way I could. I would explain how bigger business works, I would demonstrate how they needed to think and how they should show up at meetings, how to better showcase their solutions, how they needed to create services and build commercial models to augment their basic offers.

I explained how to express the value of what they did better - explain the value proposition and build business cases. The importance of case studies in selling. I would pave the way for them in whatever way I could. I'd introduce them to the right people. Helping them with their network is exactly what a young start up needs. I've always found that good people know good people; that's how our network (Black Book) flourishes.

These connections and the interconnected capability that it enabled was always easy to undervalue. Spotting something relevant that could then be connected to a client's brand meant that we could do something that had never been done before. What we built each time would become a case study, and it would get the business visibility. In turn that would get them more money from VCs (venture capitalists) and Angel investors. They would get leverage by being associated with the brand Ogilvy. We'd make a film and put it forward for awards.

Ingenuity - Or "How an Intrapreneur Does Cannes"

The Cannes Lion Innovation Festival of Creativity is a must for any innovator, but anyone who goes the regular way just isn't getting the best experience. At most conferences and festivals of this sort, people buy their tickets hoping for the chance to mingle with the geniuses in the field, but the real geniuses aren't even there.

They're having drinks with their clients or they're meeting in their bungalows across the street. If you go in the front door, you have to know you're not getting the real experience. An intrapreneur will find other ways to get the experience, ways that are often cheaper and more exciting. All the gems are in between and around the edges, that's where the real learning happens, and where the Rough Diamonds are hiding.

When I go to the Cannes Festival, I get a six-bed apartment for 1,000 Euros, and then I rent out the beds to my friends and for 250 Euros for the week.

Cannes would need to be in the diary if we were going to make the most of networking and increase the amount of great relationships for the Black Book. If it was not possible to get the money together in the usual way, then an intrapreneur must think differently. It is not done in the usual traditional ways. The value may be relevant a few years from when you first met that person in Cannes. Trusted and authentic relationships are everything

Really, though, the story shows the different mindsets of people in the corporate machinery and unlimited budgets, versus those who have to scrap for every dollar to make something happen. No matter how much better the experience and value that can be gained by playing at the bleeding edges.

Thoughts from the edge are always more inspiring. For me, the people at the edge are more inspiring too. People said Tel Aviv could never be a city because it was bog land, so the Israelis planted eucalyptus trees. The best solutions are simple. That's entrepreneurial thinking: spotting a problem and finding simple solutions. As Dave Trott continuously says, *"Simple is smart. Complicated is stupid."*

I had a call where someone wanted me to talk about creative hacking, and I told him the story of this guy called Pablo, who was a hacker about ten years ago. He did a presentation where he showed a picture of a hotel room, and he annotated around it, showing what a normal person would see: the bed, the balcony and so on. Then he said, *"But I walk into the room as a hacker and I see this:"* and he circled the TV. He then proceeded to tell us what he can do as a hacker. He could add porn to somebody's account, take money out of someone else's – we were all floored.

A few years later, I heard this guy Moran Cerf on The Moth talking about robbing a bank. He's a hacker working for a bank and he told the story of how he robbed the bank physically, not on the computer. Then he tells a whole story of how he goes on to be a neuroscientist and hacks the brain – it's amazing.

So, you can hack a hotel room and you can hack the brain, and then there's this guy who hacked his own body. He did a presentation where he's all wired up – his head, his heart, everything and you can see things going off the charts with angst and sweatiness.

You can chart the history of hacking and use it to show that some jobs are going to be lost, but they will be replaced with new jobs, jobs that are coming out of the hacking mindset. The hacking mentality can be applied to everything from finance, to your body, to your brain. If you think about it, hacking is really all about finding out how things work so you can modify them to your benefit, which is analogous to innovation in some ways.

Recently, I caused a bit of stir on LinkedIn. My daughter Claudia was filling out all these applications for internships and fellowships, and my God, they are a load of rubbish. They each take an hour, and they're full of ridiculous questions like, *"If you were a biscuit, what kind of biscuit would you be and why?"* Now, I happened to know the CEO of one of the companies she was applying to, so I called him up and asked about his hiring process. He looked for Claudia's application, and he found it with an HR guy in Burundi. It made me so mad: there are so many talented young people trying to enter the workforce, and they've got this old-fashioned HR way of doing things that just contributes to the hiring of the same old cookie-cutter candidates. She recently went for an interview for a role as a media planner, which was around strategic thinking. The HR people had her take a math test. She left Leeds University with a first-class degree. She hadn't looked at that kind of math since her GCSE's, age 16. She failed the test and didn't get the job. They didn't see this amazing kid and what she did have going for her. They had always done it that way, had always given them a math test. Even if it wasn't relevant or necessary. In my opinion, and obviously, I may be a little biased, they missed out on an incredible girl. You see, there are changes that need to be made everywhere, it isn't just about technology changes. The world is continuously changing.

I posted about Claudias experiences of finding a job on LinkedIn, and this guy wrote back to me and said he'd felt the same way, and he's started a company to combat it. (There's another example of institutional inertia leading to innovation taking place outside of organizations rather than within it.)

I met this guy Nick, who's was 22 at the time and the CEO of a startup that's working to end the ridiculous hiring process. He's an Oxford guy who went to Beijing as part of his Chinese studies. He needed money, so he set up a company in Beijing to teach English to very wealthy Chinese people's kids. He got all his friends from England, who were working pub jobs for six pounds an hour, to come and teach for him. He's 22 years old! When he came back, he started up another company to combat hiring practices.

Now, the hiring process is certainly part of retaining great talent, but there's more to it. Another key part of retaining talent is allowing communication within an organization to allow for those at the bottom to speak to those at the top. In many cases, top executives have no idea what's happening on the ground – they just can't, given the size of their company. But it's down there in the weeds where innovation is happening, and there must be a way for those lowly interns or young professionals to feel that their ideas are being heard and considered at the top. (One could argue, in fact, that a one of the great zeitgeists of our time is the groundswell of the people's voices demanding to be heard. The recent Women's March is a good example, but so is social media: if you don't allow for the democratization of access, access will be demanded in ways you might not prefer.)

A third aspect of retaining talent is working with the millennial attitude towards work, instead of against it. I often see folks putting millennials down for their work habits, but if you accept it and harness it, you can retain young creatives within the agency rather than forcing them into the startup environment. One way that I found to retain millennial workers was through the Lab Rats program. Whenever I was planning a Lab day, I'd bring in, say, twelve youngsters from all across Ogilvy, and I'd have them work as a team to prepare for and support the Lab. It gave them a chance to not only get a break from the monotony of their day jobs but also to witness the innovative work going on in the Lab. My gosh, they added so much more value to their teams and most of all their clients - as their learnings went through the roof. Before that, they didn't know what they didn't know. Their self-esteem rose, and they felt empowered to do a way better job and importantly, ask questions.

You see, much of the criticism of the Millennial workforce isn't actually a problem with them, but with their educations. They've been told all throughout their lives to sit down, shut up and do as they're told, so they get into the workforce with all the naughty energy beaten out of them. They're afraid to voice their ideas. They're scared to go against the grain. And yet they're just bursting with innovative thinking, if only we give them the resources to explore.

People always ask me why I'm so comfortable giving away my ideas, but my problem has never been people stealing my projects. In fact, it's quite the opposite. I can shout my ideas from the mountain tops, but because there's such a distinct lack of doers, very few people will go and do anything with them. Still, one of the six benchmarks of a successful intrapreneur is giving back, and openness is an end in itself.

Responsibility is not about charity, and it's not about corporate social responsibility. Rather, responsibility is a critical component of how we can measure success when ROI (return on investment) falls short as a measuring stick. Responsibility can be understood as having two aspects: paying it forward and giving it back.

For example, mentoring is one way that I have consistently measured my success as both an intrapreneur and an entrepreneur. During my music semester, I partnered with the Media Sandbox in Bristol. The Media Sandbox was run by Clare Reddington and was partly funded by the government, and they fund innovative projects. I collaborated with the Media Sandbox to support this guy who was working on creating a new musical instrument. It was a nine-month program. There was an initial brief that was answered by various people who were from academia, technology and creative industries. A conceptual idea was approved by a *Dragons Den* style group of people.

Once the idea had been approved, then they needed the mentors to help them deliver the project. To have three totally diverse types of people working together to make something truly innovative happen. When I first mentored Adam and his group, they had shown me a plastic round ball sphere shape, with plastic cups stuck into it. Each month I would be available to the team to help them progress. To think about their business model. To introduce them to the correct people to move their idea along. To give them wisdom around the business of marketing. Usually the partnerships were lacking in a certain aspect of strength. Sometimes their business acumen was missing. Sometimes the tech backup was not strong enough. It was about recognizing these things quickly and helping them move forward seamlessly, along quite a rocky road. It was because of the Labs, that Adam and his team were able to access the right people to turn his idea into a viable product. It helped me learn about the musical world, and it allowed me to tick the Responsibility box so that I could prove the semester of learning was a success.

Adam developed his product and showcased it at our music Lab day. He was introduced to the right people at this event. He started shipping his product soon after and is hugely successful. As part of our Semesters of Learning on music, we held an amazing music festival in the Ogilvy offices. Three enormous stages around the building. That were live streamed simultaneously. That had around six incredible artists performing on each stage. From Sophie Ellis Bexter to Newton Fawlkner. Each stage taken over by a major music producer. We had several stages around the floors and showcased both bands as well as future ways of consuming music. Spotify and Last FM were there. Not the major players in the music scene. Not the EMI's or Sony's. But the partners from the Black Book doing interesting innovative work in the music industry - pushing the boundaries. We wanted Adam and his new musical instrument startup company to showcase there. His company was called Alphasphere. A successful product and company was born at our music semester of learning. He now performs on the world stages.

Another great example is with Kerry, when we met at Ogilvy's Ideas Shop. I talk about that a little further down. Our initial meeting would lead us to eventually doing the most wonderful IBM big data 3D printing project. She became a trusted, respected supplier in this innovative and extremely new space. We would pay her company, 3D Printshow, as a supplier, just like you would pay a production company to do a TV commercial. These little companies would get paid by a brand, or the Lab at times, to do something they'd never done before. They might have talked about it, but they'd never actually done it. It would then give them a viable product that they could tout around and say, *"this is what we did with Ogilvy."* It was a win-win: they would be able to get their money from either Angel or VC investment and the Labs became an integral part of the ecosystem of companies. We had at least two of these case studies each year, for the last ten years, where startups or small to medium enterprises would have a tangible case study to share that had been produced with a big brand like Ogilvy and their blue-chip clients.

I'm always trying to find entrepreneurial ways to make money, so when I see a great company, I want to put money into it. But the problem is, when we do that, it's seen as a conflict of interest under the Sarbanes-Oxley Act. With Kerry's 3D Printshow for instance, the Labs were able to sponsor in a small way. Whether it be to create an event app for their kickoff event six years ago to giving away a few 3D printers to a winner of 3,000 school entries who would create the best CAD drawing, to sponsoring a 3D printed food kitchen at their last event. This helped the event get started; just like the Labs helped many others get started. It was our role and it worked.

By seeing who was out there, then attaching them to business or to the Lab semester and the Lab days, introducing them to people and brands that they ordinarily would never get to meet was seen even seventeen years ago as revolutionary. Now it is under the umbrella of the word *"innovation."* That word for me purely means, quicker, better, stronger, faster.

WPP Group Plc. has its own mergers and acquisitions, tries hard to align them and introduce the companies purchased into their portfolio of agencies. M&C Saatchi have done well with Saatchi Invest and The Bakery. By now, many are pulling together their programs to work way better with the startup communities, incubators and accelerators. Most agencies do not have it within their organizations. It is not short term enough for their finance directors so it is created as a separate entity. Like the people at Zag, which is part of BBH, they had to push it to one side; it's not actually within the company. I believe all these incubators, accelerators and startups are a response to the regulatory environment.

The other notable regulation is the Jobs Act. It allows for more private funding and total number of shareholders in a company before they have to go public or file with the SEC. As a result, there were very few IPOs (initial public offerings) in the US, but there was a ton of funding taking place for startups, both those that were just getting their first round of funding as well as more established startups like Uber, which has raised billions of dollars.

Israel is a great breeding ground for startups. The tax situation there makes it much easier to be one. In some ways, the whole country is like one big Silicon Valley. Part of it is the culture, because everyone goes through the military means they often come out with the kind of closeness you develop from experiencing perilous situations, the trust in working relationships is almost implicit. Indeed, many Israeli startups are run like military operations.

The book *Start-Up Nation* covers this. It's about how a small, brand new country like Israel can become a superpower. *Start-Up Nation* attributes the country's success to the conscription system. It also references the nonhierarchical nature of the Israeli army, because you can have fast food workers giving orders to top bankers. When I started the Labs, I used that concept of the nonhierarchical workplace.

One example of the clash of company management clashing with the scrappy, entrepreneurial spirit is with John Sculley got rid of Steve Jobs. Sculley never respected or understood what it was like to be a founder.

Problem: Not being allowed to affect change.

Solution: Prove by doing. Gather great people around you and build the Black Book.

11

HOW TO INNOVATE SUCCESSFULLY:
THE SEMESTERS OF LEARNING

the demands for innovation

78	23	18	3
% of companies with innovation goals as a part of business plans	% of companies have a dedicated team assigned to innovation	% of companies have a specific innovation budget to find new solutions	% of companies with innovation budgets view those funds as a priority

*I*t's hard to innovate within a corporate structure. Resilient structures are just that, resilient and resistant to external forces.

They are not designed for innovation. Large organizations tend to suffer from institutional inertia.

It's hard to turn a really big ship. But during my career I've hunted out all the tools I could find and kept all the ones that worked. I've built a toolbox for people trying to innovate within corporations. Below I have highlighted a few exciting examples of Semesters of Learning to give you the real story of how to make something big happen twice a year.

I have a love - hate relationship with the word innovation. I always ask people what they mean by it. And in any single team there will be multiple definitions. The same goes for the other vague words like transformation and change.

Leaders in a business will always say they want change. But they don't tend to allocate any budget for it. In my experience, when there's no budget line, there's no people. That equates to zero capability for the task at hand. If it happens to be your task, then you can be forgiven for scratching your head about how the hell you will get it done.

No one in business would deny that meaningful change demands investment. It needs investment both commercially and in people. This also goes for engagement by the enterprise. If individuals aren't given the motivation to engage then they won't. If the value isn't made clear they won't go in that direction.

One simple example of this is attendance at events. If it is free to attend an event, then most people won't bother. The minority (the more curious ones) will attend. They will always seek more and more knowledge and experience.

The difference between change and no change is often small but that makes it hard to deliver. It's mostly behavioral and based on long term habits. It's famously hard to innovate within a corporate structure.

Organizations are not designed for innovation. Instead, they are programmed to resist it. Large organizations tend to suffer from institutional inertia. It's also a fact that it's super hard to turn a really big ship. And during my career I've hunted out all the tools I could find and kept all the ones that worked.

I've built a toolbox for people trying to innovate within corporations. Below I've illustrated a few cases to give you a practical taste of how we've made change work and how that showed up. Some of these were stealthy and covert, some were more direct, but they all came from bringing the best resources to bear on real applications. I've wrapped this chapter up with the eighteen things* that run through it all.

*The 18 points below are a set of lessons that I learnt the hard way over the last decade and a half. The insights and cases all came from the Semesters of Learning and became the basis of this wealth of understanding.

The Case Of The Measure Of Pleasure

This one came out of the "Storytelling Semester." A big part of our role was to turn serendipity into a science. It was clear (to any of us that were properly involved) that innovation is never that exact. There's the challenge. In an agency, especially a large and financially focused one, it always had to have a thoroughly defensible business case. That takes great patience and a steely determination.

Successful innovation therefore takes practice and patience. Great ideas may only appear once we've exhausted all other avenues. They most certainly don't happen overnight and are not grabbed off of a shelf.

Innovation doesn't happen on a schedule, and it isn't easily measured. Not surprisingly we relied on the 6 'R's to quantify success. Identifying the metric that will get a project across the line is vital. The 6 'R's worked especially when value wasn't necessarily immediately visible.

To those with a mind wired to finances we needed to bring the (financial) conversations around to (real world) value by association. For example - on the surface of it we could never have justified sending Will Harvey, (our then Lab Creative Technologist) to IAB which was an annual event in Amsterdam, similar to CES in Vegas each year. It was all about technology and hardware and the latest and greatest gadgets. At that time it was a pretty random and *"out there"* event, and on the surface it had nothing to do with advertising.

We sent him anyway, and told him to look for anything related to storytelling. This was a fundamental Lab requirement for each semester - find interesting and cool people, identify startups, tech companies and bring them back. This way we can translate the value and importance of it to the wider agency.

On one occasion he found a guy who was doing something really interesting with stories and electroencephalogram (EEG – a method to record brain activity). It was a truly innovative and yet small company, run by Tre Azam it was called Myndplay. Tre would have you put the EEG headset around your head, like a headband

and then a video with about six different endings would play. Depending on how you felt about the character, you'd keep the character alive or keep him running.

Will brought the guy back to London and we did a Lab lunch. One of the creatives working on a chocolate brief asked, *"Is it possible to measure the pleasure of chocolate?"* Our new protégée said, *"well, I don't see why not!"* The measure of pleasure campaign was born.

Boom. The kind of moment I live for. Two amazing creatives spring the idea of measuring pleasure. A creative idea that became the campaign itself. We know how much we love to eat chocolate, what if there was an actual metric of just how much pleasure we got?

At first, we just wanted the math - could that be a marketer's dream? We all thought so. Imagine a science fiction experiment with electrodes and people in white masks wandering about clamping headsets onto our specimens' heads. Imagine them in various states of pleasure. One of them eating a little chocolate drop, another stroking an adorable puppy. Yes, it's advertising.

So, together with our partners at Ravensbourne we filmed the lot. You could literally see the result of pleasure on the screens - a bone-fide index of pleasure!

We put a little of our Labs R&D money behind it to prove it could work. The agency also put money into it and the client - who was Beyond Dark bought into the campaign. I remember, even on the day we did the experiment, everyone was really worried, as it hadn't been done before. Courage!

If you have the right people who all want the same thing then it can just happen, you just have to trust. I trusted everyone involved, especially Tre and the creative team, Graham and James.

It was their vision that we took from an idea to an incredible and award-winning reality. Sainsburys, a major UK supermarket chain took on the product and that led to many new flavors of the chocolate drops - success. Via the EEG we could literally see what it actually, felt like to eat dark chocolate drops. We all saw what it felt like to eat a competitor's chocolate.

We could observe what it felt like to blow bubbles and what it felt like to receive money in envelopes. These headsets were placed in the physical Lab space at the agency and as a result everyone could see how it worked and get hands on playing around and experimenting with all the kit.

Armed with our measurements and our films, the campaign kicked off. As we saw it working, we got even more PR involved. Eventually it became a campaign all around the world. We could eventually place a pleasure measure on the packaging.

What started as a laboratory experiment to get the science became something that stood on its own. The research became the campaign. It was a beautiful thing.

We'd involved Birkbeck University, we had filmed it and we had found that we really could measure pleasure. We could show how people reacted when they tasted chocolate or held kittens or puppies. We would never have made that amazing film if there hadn't been the idea and then the determination to send Will to what many people would consider a random event. A traditional Finance

Director would never have let that happen.

The Case Of 3D Printing And Big Data

Before the Data and 3D Printing Semester of Learning, the agency had produced a few wonderful Ideas Shops - these were initiated by a chap called Dave Birss and Ruth Jamieson in the Creative Department.

Kerry Marks, who I had mentioned in the previous chapter, had an appointment at one of these Ideas Shops. Like many of us, we were happily giving away our time for free for the pop-up shops. I mentored Kerry and stayed close to her throughout and we remain good friends to this day and still work together.

It was during an Ideas Shop that Kerry sat down to talk about some help for her upcoming business.

I asked her to close her Mac and look at her - *"let's just have a proper chat."* Kerry was always a terrific entrepreneurial spirit. She wanted to do events and a whole raft of different things, but she didn't know how.

A few weeks later I met a guy called Evan, who ran an incredible digital installation company called Seeper. We were talking about an innovative job for Ford. It involved a 3D mapping projection onto two buildings. One of them being The Senate House in London.

What Goes Around And All That

Evan was with a gentleman named Robin Dhara and they were producing the first ever TEDx event in London. They were both so overwhelmed with the event (on top of both their day jobs) and needed immediate help.

I said, *"I've got just the girl for you."* I connected him with Kerry. She killed it for him, absolutely killed it.

The next thing I know, I get a call from my friend Katz Kiely, who, at that time was working for the UN and their event for 10,000 called ITU. Putting it simply it was around global telecommunications and innovative tech. She phones me, *"Nic, I've got Kerry here, who knows you."*

What had happened was Katz had gone to Evan's London TEDx event. She had said to Evan, *"My God, I'm really having a nightmare - this show is enormous, and I really need more help."* He says, *"I have just the girl for you."* And he gave Kerry to Katz.

A Net Result

As a result, Kerry sees directly all of the stuff going on with 3D printing, and she decides to set up a 3D printing showcase.

Also, as a direct consequence Kerry knew I was in need of a 3D printer in the physical space of the Innovation Lab. The Labs had given her much guidance through her 3D print show event, so she gave us some 3D printers, free of charge. This inspired the creatives within the agency, having such an amazing piece of kit in their hands within the Lab. This was at a time when few people really knew what a 3D printer was.

The creative team, working on IBM Wimbledon, began playing with the new 3D printer. They began asking questions about their own creative idea. And we were off again. But that's another case study, from another Semester.

Kerry's next show was a VR(virtual reality) show for 10,000 people in London, covering VR within medical, defense, entertainment, education, sports and fashion. I worked closely with her as a partner on it. We curated VR across all brand segments of the show.

In all, that's seven or eight years of a relationship. All the stuff underneath the iceberg. Yes, we see the success, but now you can see how it actually happened.

The Black Book works because there are no demands. There's no expectation and there's no obligation. It's about paying it forward. I never expected anything when I mentored Kerry and connected her to all those people and opportunities.

It's just what we do!

The Case of Flooding Second Life

During the Virtual World "Semester of Learning" I met Kathryn Parsons. She was a Fellow at the agency. One day she came to me quite upset, saying, *"I don't know what I'm going to do. I don't know how to make this happen!"* I said, *"We need to be calm and think straight - stay with the facts, be logical and get the right people working together. This is going to be fine. We're going to do this one step at a time."*

We did. We worked together to flood Second Life the Virtual World. First of all, I encouraged her to showcase the idea. One of the foundational roles of an intrapreneur is to help others shine, so I insisted she showcase the work.

She talked at events for the APA (Advertising Producers Association) and at BAFTA (British Academy of Film and Television Arts) to showcase the flooding of Second Life. This was in front of around 500 people. She did brilliantly and gained enormous amounts of confidence. She went on to found Decoded.

On the same project was Giles Ryse Jones, who was part of a tiny start up called What3Words. We worked closely at this time and especially in the early days of the Labs. He was all over digital and we were the ones, along with a great lady named Olivia who eventually pulled it off.

When he left the agency (in similar circumstances to myself), we met up at Shoreditch House. We sat for a few hours and I helped him develop his own Black Book. We discussed who he should chat to about this new start up, what events should he showcase or speak at.

It wasn't about what I would get in return it was what could I do for a good person. I gave him all of the events he must go to, all the contacts he needed. What3Words became famous - they were recently at South by Southwest where I was judging the innovation awards. It made me smile to judge them.

FREGGO - Case Study

Visualization Semester of Learning

The Freggo project was an interesting one. It really was all about the art of the possible. It was something that had never been seen before and was pure ingenuity. We created an art installation using data visualization and that was the central focus for what we described as a *"Sensational Ice Cream"* campaign.

At the time, this was a new UK brand called Freggo. The brand was a new venture from the owners of Gaucho - the chain of

Argentinian restaurants. It was a genuine innovation in media and way ahead of its time. It was all based on a computer program that captured six core elements of ice cream flavors. The response data (sweetness, richness, creaminess, juiciness and so on) were fed into the program to define how the visuals themselves would look. It was called Taste and that was what it was all about!

The installation was built and the public were invited to view it at the Menier Gallery in Southwark in central London. It was an incredible moment. The creative team at the time included Rae Stones and Fiona Sanday and they worked with Andrew Shoben from Greyworld, an art collective.

Behind this we had to work really hard to make it happen and create a conducive environment for great work to emerge. Artists need to work in a particular way and that way is unique to them.

"You can never have too much work if you're an artist and looking for commissions. You always live with the fear that was your last project, no matter how successful you get."
- Andrew Shoben. Greyworld

Working with agencies can be difficult so one of my challenges was to give the talent a fair shot. It's not easy making a smooth process between a big global agency and an individual artist. The conflict arises because the role of the agency is to protect the relationship with its client whilst also creating a good working relationship with the artist. On top of that, making that all work with the client as well.

The agency will come up with the brief and introduce an artist to it. At this point, the agency has to show its strength. Can we manage the project, nurture the idea, keep the artist on track and develop the idea and improve on it as we go?

In many situations they can't. Not only do they have difficulty creating the idea in the first place, they are also unhappy letting a third party do their thing. This happens all the time. It's a delicate balance working your way through that. We knew that Andrew could add serious value, but we needed to get the chemistry right to make this work properly.

I knew Greyworld and I had the confidence they would do a brilliant job. They had been making public art for a long time and we needed people who knew what it would take. We definitely wouldn't want to take the risk with our client.

At the end of the day I knew we could rely on Andrew. He formed the group when he was 18. They were used to making their own decisions, working in teams, and choosing what to do next. In practical terms it meant they understood collaboration well and how vital that would be with the complexity of a project like this.

"A vital part of collaboration is knowing where not to collaborate – where individual experts should do their thing, and then regroup and see how it all fits in. And if it needs changing, change it. It's exactly like making a film - it's a dance of experts, focusing on their part of the puzzle and then listening to constructive feedback, respectfully and with an open mind."
- Andrew Shoben. Greyworld

The Case Of The Fanta Stealth Sound System

The Mobile Semester of Learning

This is a great case of where crazy connections can make magic happen. Martyn Ware is the founder of Illustrious and also the founder of Human League and Heaven 17. Illustrious creates all sorts of applications for two-dimensional sound, and sound composition in general. They do it for all sorts of applications.

We met initially around ten years ago at The Museum of Sound and Industry in Manchester. Martyn did a soundscape for an event called b.tween. It was a revolutionary digital event, run by, my now close friend, Katz Kiely. This soundscape was a kind of sonic heat map of people's interactions in the entire space. It was a really incredible experience to witness. A 3D soundscape inside a conference space that showed how people were interacting within the space.

Our brief was from Fanta - quite simply to do something special and different. We had come up with some ideas and this one was more different than most. Our solution was a mobile application for teenage ears only! Think about that.

Our idea was to use a frequency of sound that only travels a small distance and give teenagers (our target audience) a tool which was their private thing. At the time Martyn's and my children were entering their teenage years and the guiding idea was to push towards something that they would they find cool?

"Being a bit naughty in class or being able to communicate where the teacher couldn't spot it or recognize it is a fun and subversive idea. Subversive ideas lead to creativity - and creativity leads to greater engagement and awareness."

I asked Martyn if he would be interested in our project at least two years after I met him at that event. His name and number were in my Black Book. I remembered that he was also working with RFID tags. Martyn had RFID tags built into the conference passes which linked to software that detected when two tags around people's necks within a meter of each other. At that point it created the effect of a three-dimensional sound in space. As the signals reached the server it generated a sound within the soundscape in the central hall. As that all built up over time it became like a scrolling piano roll. Over time it built up and built up.

Our whole solution was based on the same technology used to deter teenagers from hanging around outside shops and bus shelters. Originally it was called the Mosquito Teen Repellent and developed by Howard Stapleton.

Our solution became known as the Fanta Stealth Sound System. Put simply, it used high-pitched frequencies, only audible to the under 20's. It included wolf-whistles, warnings, psst's and sound tags for phrases like *"cool"*, *"uncool"*, and *"let's get out of here."*

Martyn then developed the soundtags, XS2 The World developed the application, and our creatives at the time - Mike Watson and Jon Morgan, together with creative partner Alasdair Graham created the campaign.

On the back of that Coca-Cola Europe launched a second mobile application, Fanta Virtual Tennis and a 3D Augmented Reality tennis game created by The Hyperfactory.

The insight in all this was that our hearing declines with age. It was almost unbelievable to the leaders of the agency that this would even work. I remember well when the sounds were played during a presentation of the idea to the board that none of the oldies heard any of them.

Meeting people in a random way always bears fruit. Maybe not at the time but almost always serendipity plays its card! Martyn would ordinarily never have crossed an ad person's path.

We were both networkers but had developed hard earned principles for any interaction and number one was always to be nice to everyone. We both believe in the value of a meaningful connection. We both had a Black Book but that would have been meaningless without knowing the people who you can work with.

Before the project, I phoned Martyn up and said do you want to come into the agency and take a brief from the creatives? Martyn wasn't initially comfortable working with advertising agencies. He was reticent. He had been burnt a couple of times by agencies who had wanted to use his expertise without really giving any credit or financial reward. There are unfortunately many people out there that are willing, and not that shy about sucking people knowledge dry and owning it themselves to impress their bosses.

For the right reasons Martyn trusted me. And we went and did it. Both of us shared a personality trait that says that if someone says it can't be done, we both respond with a *"oh really?"*

It worked, the project was a huge success. The agency and most importantly the client were extremely happy. They loaded the website and downloaded the sounds onto all Fanta cans. We stopped counting once it hit one million downloads.

Martyn was thrilled. The campaign was awarded, and Martyn's name was on it. It was one of the early jobs where collaboration was key, and we could prove it. It was not just an agency idea or a production company idea or a director or an illustrator, but it was a true co-creation.

Genuinely working with others.

When the Labs closed it was a shock for everyone. Martyn made the point that there should be many more people like those of us in the Lab. They are the oil in the engine of the creative industry or grit in the oyster to create the pearl.

You have to focus on the best people and trust them to do the job properly. If they don't do the job properly then you have a problem. This problem will need to be negotiated and worked out, but that's the most efficient way of organizing people.

Team LAB

Probably the most important case of all - What did it teach us?

Throughout my life and now written in this book are the life lessons that informed me. They were all wrapped up in the team that was formed. It was built from scraps, guile and belligerence. These things and great people came together to make the Labs the success it was.

There're many more examples but these are will give you a glimpse of how innovation can work. Against the odds. Never a sponsored program with neat edges.

1. **Something From Nothing** - Making something happen from nothing. Literally nothing. No space, no place, no budget, and no time to prove value. Break rules. Ask for forgiveness.

2. **The Qualities Of A Team** - I couldn't have written the brief for the perfect team without my life's lessons. My base instinct was for a team filled with people of quality. These qualities: honesty and integrity, keeping promises, thinking broadly and thinking ahead, care for the task and sincerity in delivering it, respecting external partners as much as internal agency folk, knowing the *"Black Book."*

3. **A Team Is Never One Person** - Yes, they were a dream team. But nothing would have been done if I had been on my own. To start it was myself and two wonderful assistants Joanne Bloom and Ruth McCarthy - never underestimate the power of personal assistants. Great personal assistants are worth their weight in gold, they always know the right people and how to make things actually happen.

4. **If You Want Something Done Ask Busy People** - As we started to build, we were hugely reliant on the Lab Rats as they were affectionately known. Always curious Lab Rats. We were all busy, focused and passionate - about pretty much everything. In those early days there was a lot to do to get the Lab knocked into shape and working efficiently. Our audience didn't really know what we were going to be doing. There was no time to wait and see, so we had to build and deliver value both at the same time. Quite a trick to pull off.

5. **Understanding The Art Of Leverage** - It was about being ingenious with small amounts of resources and making maximum impact. We called it alchemy. We made precious material out of base metals. Our antennae was always up. Stuff that was just lying around was commandeered and put to better use. It was the same with the team. As Joanne moved on to another role Shannon Vaughan, originally starting as my assistant, went on to take on the Rough Diamond program as a fully-fledged Lab role. She took to the role like a duck to water. She worked closely with our original and first official Rough Diamond - Will Harvey.

6. **Build It and They Will Innovate** - Will looked after our physical Lab space - by now it was enormous. It had grown exponentially. The more we found out about the possibilities for innovation the more we brought it in to feed the creativity. The more we fed the creativity, the more it drove us to push innovation to new edges.

7. **Stay Inspired Even On The Red-Eye** - I was becoming even more of a pioneer into digital. The more curious I became the more inspired I was. I was learning everything I could about the digital world. I went to every lecture, every seminar and every workshop I could find. There was so much happening and there was so much value in what I could bring back to the Lab.

8. **Sharpening The Filter** - Every meeting meant new connections and I learnt to hone my instincts. What would work? What wouldn't? Who were good people and who were the bad? One day after getting back from Arizona, I found a large meeting room at Ogilvy that had my name all over it. It seemed to be shouting out *"fill me with value!"* . But be darned sure what that means. Because no matter how brilliant it is someone will want to kill you for it. And that's not a good thing.

9. **Be Sure You Cultivate The Great Leaders And The Stupid Rules** - Paul O'Donnell gave me the thumbs up to that Lab

space when I got back from the US. He got what we were doing and why it was valuable. Given the strange vagaries of accounting policy a meeting room meant that I wouldn't need to find money to pay for it. It was paid for by *"facilities."* That meant, I could also call it a Lab, but most importantly not have to pay anything for it. Will immediately started wiring it up. It would soon be a Digital Innovation Lab. Facilities would no doubt wander by every day with their clipboard. Nobody died.

10. **Bringing The Outside In** - Once it started to take shape, we contacted many of the people we had met at the seminars or during the Semesters. These were wonderful people. We knew they sold and developed truly great digital equipment but didn't have showrooms. They were the makers, the digital craftsmen and women. This technology was exploding, and the Labs gave us a way to create a mutual place to showcase their work and find business opportunities for them.

11. **Creating The Real Meaning Of Mutual Value** - We didn't have a budget for purchasing any of this technology, so it made complete sense to create real mutuality. We could get bleeding edge technology into the hands and heads of our creatives for zero cost. Our new partners could have the space in the agency for free. They would supply and maintain the equipment between 12pm to 2pm daily, they could use the space to demonstrate it. As far as the accountants were concerned, it was a meeting room. That meant we just always booked it out for meetings. That was how we worked around the rules. We were already excellent at that.

12. **Taking It To The Streets** - Our strategy was to get close to everyone in the building who would understand the value of what we brought to the table. We would need ambassadors to stay ahead. We educated those that could see what that value was. We would need a majority of people to be on the side of the Labs. Although, partly that would be by

giving them access to fresh ideas and all the utility of the new technologies they would also need to value us, the team. They genuinely did. And they do to this day.

13. **Identify the Doers** - We became close allies with all the doers in the agency, the people in the organization responsible for making product. We covered everyone and made no distinction of job role. It was about finding the quality people, from the receptionists who were always greeting the new partners, to the IT guys to help Will with the fixing, to the facilities teams who were always helping us out.

14. **Turning Collaboration, Into A Currency** - It really worked. It was true collaboration and value for everyone. To me this is the best definition of return of investment (ROI). Even though we all made the investment, the agency always got the return. The agency got literally hundreds of thousands of pounds worth of return. They got insight and competitive advantage and the use of unique and expensive equipment. They got it for free. Our partners got a great place to showcase their technology alongside real cases and in front of the agency's global clients. The team always thought like entrepreneurs. We felt it was our own little business. We made stuff happen.

15. **From Little Acorns** - Later on and always as a team we started working more with Rory Sutherland and Jez Groom together with a new joiner Dan Bennett. This was with a brand-new offering around behavioral change. Will, Shannon and now Tamsin Dace a new assistant became a formidable team. We managed to infiltrate the group companies and really make progress - we really kicked some ass. For the very first time we all felt like we had become a bona fide department, of sorts. The London Lab was the place everyone was talking about. People were wanting to work with us - internally and externally.

16. **Becoming A Power** - In some ways it was ironic. We were definitely a brand within a brand. Because of what we were

doing, we were suddenly the cool ones doing the cool stuff. Not everyone likes that. They didn't see the value we saw. We soldiered on, what else could we do. There're always the naysayers. Many people took no time to even understand. People who should have known better. People who know value and what we did could see it, we were bringing vital information back to the agency and making it accessible to anyone who wanted it.

17. **Test And Learn And Then Test Again. The World Is Then Yours** - Our team and our Semesters of Learning became synonymous with cutting edge advantage. Each new semester would encourage around ten curious people, usually fellows who wanted to engage and help. One of the semesters was for IOT (internet of things). One super smart account executive, who was working on the American Express account put up her hand to say she wanted to work on that with the Labs. Her name was Gemma Milne and she was super smart, young, enthusiastic and we connected immediately. It was like I had found a missing link. She could translate what I wanted to say to the management and account teams, she spoke their language.

18. **All Good Things And All That** - And so it was that when Will left for pastures new at a company called VCCP as their head of innovation it was a natural fit to have Gemma take his place. This was a more strategic role that involved significant research and development. Continuing on with all the alchemy associated with our approach, our previous year's Rough Diamond Jack took on all the tech and the physical Lab space. (Matt Powell and Tom Sharman were to join - to make it a grand total of four people in the Lab - for just a few weeks before it was finally shut down.)

If two years from now someone needed anything, let's say some mobile gaming or AR (augmented reality) or a streaming technology, we have tangible case studies and a whole plethora of great people who can get it done. At first, it's scary and new, but at a certain point it becomes the new normal.

That's how-to bring change to a large organization. That is why the semesters were crucial. Our approach was crucial and our mentality was crucial. This was the only way it could be done. I did it this way and it worked. Different organizations will have different contexts, but the principles will be the same. My hope is that this book will give you more tools to help drive innovation forward in your organization.

Problem: Being unable to educate, inspire and do new things.

Solution: The Semesters of Learning and an amazing trustworthy team.

12

THE ROUGH DIAMOND

*I*n corporate life, you'll often hear the expression *"ask for forgiveness, not permission."* If your intention is pure, then you make something happen - something that you know needs doing for the greater good and without waiting for the OK.

This allows you to show people what you have done and accomplished. It's not that people aren't intelligent or tone deaf to the explanation, but sometimes they seem incapable of interpreting it in the right way. Also, by doing first and explaining later people will see and be able to evaluate something real. When people see, they can comprehend.

In my whole experience I've learnt to prove by doing. Nothing truly great can be accomplished by a PowerPoint presentation alone *especially* when it comes to innovation and ingenuity.

There was always an understanding that the agency needed creative talent to survive. For me, creativity went far beyond the *"creative teams."* Art and copy, the classic definitions of creativity in an agency were always far too narrow for me. I always saw just as much creativity in production and logistics, media and everything that it took to get campaigns to air. I could easily make a case that it could be more creative to develop a media plan to bring a specific campaign idea to life. Just as I saw, genius post-production and editing make quite ordinary work become award winning.

Then I would see some entirely average account directors taking below par briefs from clients and creating many hours of wasted time. I was fortunate. I'd worked at the best creative and most awarded agencies in London in the late '80's and '90's so I was able to make a good judgement call. For me, it was all about talent. How we would survive in the future would have to be about bringing fresh blood and new ideas to the table. It didn't seem that tough a thought to me.

I kept trying to persuade the senior executives that we needed to be investing in the future talent. It was an almost impossible struggle. HR said they understood, but they still did it in the same old way. In true disruptive style, we simply went around them and did it anyway.

As with many things, during these years some time later we were having lunch with the Dean of Ravensbourne, at the time, Sir Robin Baker. He was really impressed with all our work on the Rough Diamond program. He was big with praise for the scheme - the leaders were happy to take the praise. I didn't say anything, just smiled and let them have the credit. On to the next thing.

Marketers face countless challenges in today's digital age. The constant evolution of technology is only one of them. It causes a ripple of effects, changes in the consumer landscape and social innovation that changes how people think and work. The way we work can change attitudes and pave the way for greater collaboration. The issues and impacts for environmental sustainability. The massive challenges around robotics, AI and the resulting need for greater ethical controls and transparency - that's just to name a few of the biggies.

But what about the next generation of agency employees? How do we ensure that our values of originality and pervasive creativity are carried forward into the time-conscious leaders of tomorrow? This was a powerful question for me.

Generational issues cloud every industry. There's generally a major gap between leaders and their front-line employees, and that is in addition to major questions of gender and diversity.

The new generations are growing up in the information intensive age where social media platforms are as every day as the sun and the moon. They have a comfort level with new technologies that allows them to easily adapt to the accelerating level of innovation which is redefining the workplace. The leaders in many industries today are nowhere near them in terms of understanding what tools and cultures they require to perform.

As job roles and company structures change with consumer expectations and technological advances, so do the requirements of new talent. New talent is only going to come from thinking differently about where talent emerges in the first place. Either we look further into the experienced older generations and ponder what creativity is all about or we find raw material in the younger generations.

From the generational point of view, we are now referring to the newer generations (Z or Y) as the iGeneration. They are the demographic cohort after the millennials.

Many of these are already struggling through secondary schools and finding it seriously hard if not impossible to imagine a career. Many are wondering what life holds for them. Many won't make it to realize their dreams.

As job roles and company structures change with consumer expectations and technological advances, so do the requirements of new talent.

These generations are well defined through widespread use of the internet. They've been exposed to technology to a sophisticated degree and from a very young age. The irony is that they are very comfortable with technology, interacting on social media is their default way to connect and communicate with friends, but they live amid the confusion of the broader world at large. I believe the contrast between new technologies and old ways of doing things has caused some disillusionment in these younger generations.

However, it is within this generation that the future lives. I've seen hundreds of these kids and know they are incredible and creative. They just don't necessarily know it yet. I knew I could cultivate a passion within them, and I knew it could be a distinct advantage for the agency as well as doing good in the world.

With their innate technical ingenuity aside, millennials and younger generations have proved to me they could be multidisciplined as they are naturally curious about so much. Even with these inbuilt skills, they would need to learn how to apply them commercially and we would need to play our part to design the right program that way. As employers we need to ensure that we give them the best opportunity. That means real work experience and as early on as possible. I found them all to be incredibly entrepreneurial with their thinking, making something happen from nothing.

I took this mission to heart. And as an innovation hub, the Lab's primary aim was to introduce the agency, our clients and now our students to all the new and emerging technologies. Who best to help us bring all this new technology to life and make it meaningful than the new generations who were not only capable of using it but also unafraid to experiment - to be *truly* creative. It was their opportunity to feel appreciated for their intrinsic value rather than being judged by the grades they got at school. The Lab team and especially Joanne Bloom and Shannon Vaughan made sure to make them feel relevant in this scary teenage world.

Rough Diamond was an idea between Chris Thompson, Graham Hitchens and I. Chris worked at Ravensbourne and Graham held a government office position. We had a very passionate and creative conversation about new raw talent and getting fresh thinking into a big agency like Ogilvy.

It was a pleasure to work with the then Finance Directors , James Barnes Austin and Jeremy Summerfield who are both no longer in the agency. They understood the value of what we were doing. They were actually excited to be involved in such disruptive ideas and original thinking.

Our Vision For Rough Diamond Was Simple And It Was Written Down

"To diversify the talent pool entering the creative industries and to engage industry in the education of the young people who aspire to work within it.

By collaborating, a diamond shaped route into the industry is created. Harvesting, nurturing and developing young talent who have completed the program become capable of feeding back into the system to mentor the next generation of talent. Hence, a sparkling self- sustainable model is born, delivering knowledge skills and expertise to those with a passion to succeed"

The Rough Diamond Program In More Detail

The Rough Diamond Program was a collaboration between educational disrupters and innovators in educational learning who have partnered to identify, develop and nurture new creative talent. The idea was simple - to provide a new talent pool to fish in.

It would identify passionate and talented people seeking to get a foothold and career in what should be the most creative of all industries - the creative industry itself.

To us, that was a definition that embraced all the industries our clients were in. So, that was all the creative industries. Between us and Ravensbourne who did corresponding courses we covered everything from Fashion, 3D, Broadcast, Lighting, Engineering, Architecture, Advertising, Art, Crafts, Design, Film, Music, Performing Arts, Publishing, R&D, Software, Toys and Games, TV and Radio, Video Games and Data Science. By creating a program that wove these courses and our business requirements with raw talent from wherever we needed to find it we could consistently bring in the *hunters* and the entrepreneurially-minded.

The idea was to encourage them still further. We gave them space in the agency and we introduced them to our clients. We would invest in the projects that emerged. Our combined aim was to help instill yet more creativity into the curriculum. It really was about harnessing young creative talent by giving them the chance to work with *real* agencies with *real life* briefs. Bringing them into an environment that they never knew existed, they believed their future was potentially a supermarket checkout. Here were the keys to a world that would have otherwise seemed unattainable.

As a result of our intervention and support, we could then feed our two key partners with case-proven material of kids with a hunger to learn and move to the next step. First, The School of Communication Arts a student agency (16-19+ years old) with a curriculum written by the industry it serves. There are no teachers, instead it has over 450 mentors from the creative industries who give their time for free to facilitate real learning.

Second, was Ravensbourne, a University sector college (again 16-19+ years old). It has established itself as a technological hub for creatives and businesses to collaborate under the same roof. Its programs encourage collaboration on real client briefs across all media and channel disciplines.

Lastly, we had identified The Marketing Academy who run a scholarship program on the development of leadership skills for people who have been in the marketing or communications industry between 4 and 12 years.

It all worked like this; the Ideas Foundation identified students who were felt to be interested in the communications industry. They were usually the kids that were about to be expelled, or were skipping classes because the school was not able to tap into their curiosity. They became immediately eligible for specific scholarships at the School of Communication Arts (SCA). Those interested in creativity and technology were introduced to the various programs at Ravensbourne.

Because we were able to make projects and cases real with *actual* projects we could inspire and engage throughout. We would have first pick of the emerging talent from these organizations. After 4 to 12 years of working within the industry, nominations for a creative scholarship at the Marketing Academy would then be accepted for past students.

My vision was for repeating this model nationally and globally because it worked. The next step called for more employers to take ownership of skills in partnership with colleges and training providers like this.

Many more businesses across all industries need to take charge and develop training that meets their business needs. They need to ensure that the development of new skills become an integral part of business strategy whilst also being in line with the changing technology landscape.

It requires the vision and a much more integrated approach to skills-development. This means mutual value programs like Rough Diamond where colleges respond to a genuine demand. It delivers (far more economically) the immensely valuable skills which businesses are prepared to pay for. Beyond that, it is a sustainable model.

David Holloway and Angela Conway from Ideas Foundation, Marc Lewis and Adah Parris from SCA, Chris Thompson, Bob Harris, Claire Selby, Jo Eaton, Carrie and at Ravensbourne and Sherilyn Shackell from Marketing Academy all deserve a special mention. Without their vision and trust, The Rough Diamond Program would not have survived in changing many kids lives and directions and ultimately lead to the title of this book!

Rough Diamond was run brilliantly on the ground by Shannon Vaughan and then Matt Powell. It was all kicked off originally by the formidable Joanne Bloom with Will Harvey, one of our original Rough Diamonds.

Will's inspiring story of being our original Rough Diamond, goes as follows....

Rough Diamond - An Origin Story

It was early in 2009 that I first met Nicole in a professional sense (although there had been some family ties in the past). We met in a members' club not unlike Shoreditch House. After being introduced, I was scheduled to be running the Ravensborne degree show with two of my fellow broadcasting students Sam and Stuart.

It was to be the last Student Run Degree show of the old site before closing down for six months and moving to its fantastic new home on the Greenwich peninsular. In that hour and a half meeting, which was originally meant to be just 30 minutes to try get some advertising people to attend the show, we discussed a number of things from the industry, talent, creativity, technology and what innovation meant to us all.

From this session, we kicked off a relationship and program that would span several years, shaping the future of dozens of young people careers and inspired a larger audience to what the future of talent could be.

In the summer of 2009, myself and five fellow students were based in the Ogilvy Office for six months under the supervision of Jo Bloom acting as a little creative team/ agency within the Ogilvy Labs initiative. Rather than spending six months whilst our university was being moved to its new home and having a student job or earning money as a supermarket cashier, we found a new home and new output for our creative and alternative talents within Ogilvy with Nicole, Jo and the Labs.

The team was made up of creative content students, graphic designers, lighting engineers and myself a broadcasting engineering student, not the usual rabble that Ogilvy wouldn't touch with a barge pole. Regardless, we had an opportunity to work alongside existing creative teams on live briefs for a number of brands, new business pitches and presentations. Bringing our own alternative creative approach and ideas to the table, this was known as the Rough Diamond.

Over the six months, we all got exposure to so many aspects of the Ogilvy business from the inside, working on live business problems as our own little melting pot of alternative talents. At the same time being supported and pushed by the Labs team to really challenge the existing status quo.

What was unique was that we could be shoulder to shoulder with creative directors, clients and fantastic minds that is FAR from any existing Internship/Grads "Playpen" programs run by most organizations.

At the end of the program, Nicole, Jo and myself worked together to shape an ENTIRELY new role and category within Ogilvy and look to *hire me as their first ever Creative Technologist. This without a doubt was a pivotal moment for the future of not just my career, the original Rough Diamonds and the numerous years that followed.*

Who knows where we would all be now without this truly innovative program that we shaped together. The four years I then spent as a Creative Technologist within the Labs had been some of the most eye-opening and rich set of challenges and experiences I have ever seen. We worked to change Ogilvy from within as an agile R&D department looking to challenge everything and anyone. This has now been hard-coded into myself as I have moved on to becoming an Innovation Lead for another agency. This path and journey i have been on with Nicole and Labs can't really be summed up in this alone, but I know I owe my curious challenging and disruptive attitude to this.

All credit to Joanne Bloom, my amazing assistant, she took on this role like a duck to water. Think of her as the *"Mum"* to the Rough Diamonds.

She made sure she got them all totally immersed. She involved them in the whole group of companies. She organized their days and their jobs so that they knew what they would be doing in their time with us throughout the year. She encouraged them, supported them, guided them and made that first year of Rough Diamonds extremely proud to be working in such an incredible place like Ogilvy. Their pride would bring a tear to my eyes regularly because it hadn't been handed to them on a silver platter. They knew what hard work felt like. Whether they were from diverse cultures, low income, or even found academia difficult because of learning difficulties, they all had that fire in their belly to make them stand out from the crowd. These kids were going to help the agency guide its future - as long as they were encouraged and allowed to.

How utterly depressing to find that once the Lab closed down, this was going to cease to exist. Why did management not think this was the most amazing innovative idea? It's a question I continue to ask myself.

Joanne also found her incredible replacement when it came to move on. Shannon Vaughan took Rough Diamond from strength to strength, carrying on finding those incredible kids. We had seven wonderful and inspiring years making a real difference, mining for the Rough Diamonds and spreading the value throughout the Ogilvy Group.

Another one of our Rough Diamonds who came from Ideas Foundation, was Ethan Bennet - he tells a wonderful short tale about the program:

The Rough Diamond program gave me the confidence to quit university and pursue a career as an unqualified creative. You're told to get a degree your whole life, but choosing a different path, working hard and surrounding yourself with great people and mentors will take you further than any piece of paper ever will. All people want to see at the end of the day are your ideas and that you're not an arsehole.

After a couple of years of running we officially launched Rough Diamond to the world in 2012. We did it together with the Ideas Foundation at Learning Without Frontiers which was pulled together by Adah Parris. It was a conference and festival in London's Kensington Olympia that was initiated and run by Graham Brown-Martin. A true future education visionary. We wanted people to copy it, because it worked. It showed that people can have amazing ideas. We made it happen, but even if you try to give it away, people are still so busy with their day jobs that it just doesn't happen or get implemented elsewhere. Mainly because they are not measured by its success.

The event brought together disruptive thinkers, innovators and practitioners to share knowledge, ideas and experiences about new learning. That year the event featured some star speakers among many others, Noam Chomsky, Ellen Mac Arthur and of course Sir Ken Robinson.

Recruitment and Responsibility were always the most difficult of the 6 'R's to get buy-in for. Especially from the new CEO and the new Finance Director, they really couldn't ever see the value. They found it impossible to see the measure of value.

In truth, it was easy to measure, we saved the agency $66k over the years in recruitment fees and hiring talent alone. Talent that would never have joined their agency through traditional means.

By the time the Labs was shut down I seem to remember Ogilvy and their HR department had set something up called *"the pipe."* It was nothing like Rough Diamond. They were looking merely for an art director and a copywriter. Rough Diamonds were the ones who wouldn't fit into a box, the whole point was to invent new roles for the disruptive digital age of technology.

On the outside of Ogilvy there was enormous reward. Most people would talk of the way our Labs diversity program was set up so many years ago. Only now are companies putting in a diversity program. I was honored to be awarded an honorary fellowship with Ravensbourne for all the work that had been achieved in changing some of their students' lives.

The pinnacle was when Ravensbourne and Ogilvy were acknowledged for the success of our partnership and awarded Best Collaboration between a University and employer at the 2016 National Undergraduate Employability Awards. The award celebrates the most effective and influential collaborations between a university and employer to offer students additional employability skills and opportunities.

Below is a quote on The Ravensbourne Website, about the award given and the power of the relationship that was set up with Ogilvy Labs and Ravensbourne:

The collaboration between Ravensbourne and Ogilvy began in 2011 with a future talent program called The Rough Diamond, which partnered educational disrupters and innovators in educational learning with aims to identify, develop and nurture new creative talent. The project is open to second year Ravensbourne students who have the opportunity to secure a one-year internship. Ogilvy have employed 13 Ravensbourne students since the start of the collaboration and have a 50 percent hire rate at the end of each year's intake.

Ravensbourne Industry Liaison, Jo Eaton said; *"Ravensbourne and Ogilvy have been developing the Rough Diamond Program over the past six years and there are many people to thank for the program's success. It is fantastic to finally gain recognition for all the hard work of both the teams and of course to acknowledge the amazing successes of the students that have benefitted from the program."*

Nicole Yershon, Director of Innovative Solutions at Ogilvy said of the scheme, *"It has really changed the way we look at future talent. We can put these students straight to work on live briefs as they have the skill set ready to go. We wanted to immerse them in our business giving them the space to learn and grow, but also give them guidance along the way."*

The awards received over 400 nominations from employers, universities and students and the winners of each award were selected by an independent judging panel, made up of industry professionals. Ravensbourne and Ogilvy warded off competition from finalists University of East Anglia and the East of England Energy Group, EC Futures and Tata Technologies, The University of Birmingham and Capgemini, The University of Nottingham and International Celebrity Networks (ICN) and Glasgow Caledonian University, Glasgow School for Business and Society and Enterprise Rent-A-Car.

One thing to remember, in school, we're rewarded for having the answer, not for asking a good question. This may explain why kids who start off asking endless *"why"* and *"what if"* questions gradually ask fewer and fewer of them as they progress through grade school.

University and corporate culture knock divergent thinking out of you. You're taught to pass exams. You're rewarded for following instructions and penalized for trying things differently. Although, it is still possible to apply the concepts of divergent thinking within corporate culture. It was my default strategy to establishing a nonhierarchical team with as many of the crazy diamonds as I could find.

The newest plans are for a Free School, that is funded by the UK Government. It is called The Ideas College. Starting at age 14, and extending to all students who were about to be kicked out of their other schools. We will hand pick each one and give them a proper education as well as the resources they need to become intrapreneurs. The Rough Diamond program continues but in another form. It just goes to show that any attempts to stifle or disconnect innovation will hurt you many times over because innovation doesn't stop, it just takes a different form. That form might even be a competitor who ends up completely disrupting your business model.

Some parting words from Shannon Vaughan who ran the incredible Rough Diamond program after Joanne Bloom got it up and running.

"After working at Nickelodeon International, I decided I wanted to become a teacher. I had spent time with children and youth, who were feeling the pressures of after-school activities and school work in order to have the 'right' background to enter the workplace... even though some were as young as nine-years-old! So, I moved to Ogilvy to work as a personal assistant where I could still work in the creative industry but have enough time to study. It was great to work for a full-service agency, and quickly I got involved in many projects on the side because there was some great work being pushed out and I enjoyed being part of it. However, I wanted more, to find a role where I could get more involved in the work but I was getting frustrated because I was 'only a PA' and it can be difficult to transition from a PA into other roles.

Little did they know, that personal assistants are your best friends! They know everything that is going on, can multi-task like nobody's business and most importantly, know how to get shit done amidst the chaos. It was during this time that I met Nicole Yershon. Her long-time PA, Joanne Bloom, was leaving Ogilvy and she needed a replacement, big shoes to be filled as they had worked together for eight years. Nicole walked with confidence, spoke with conviction and was a force to be reckoned with. I was a little nervous and very excited! In fact, colleagues had warned me that she had a reputation and I might be tied to it if I worked with her, giving me one of those cautious nods. If nothing else, this gave me cause to find out what all the fuss was about.

My role with Nicole was three-fold:

1. *To be her PA and work on the Lab Days*
2. *To look after the physical Lab space*
3. *To run the internship program Ogilvy Labs had initiated – (plus I was still a PA for the Head of Digital. I was going to be busy)*

The beauty of this role was that I got to work in the creative industry and still work with youth; my passion that Nicole picked up on immediately. I had spent years trying to find the 'right' role, believing that I had to be able to perform the job role before I was able to get hired into it, when in actual fact all I needed to do was believe in myself. Now I got to expose youth to the creative industry and show them that they don't need to know everything, they will get trained into the role, that is why they call them entry-level roles! Quickly my life became consumed by work, reporting to two managers as a PA, assisting three account teams, managing the physical Lab space and mentoring and finding work for the youth in our program which we named the 'Rough Diamond.' Luckily, my other manager was very supportive, so was in good hands between him and Nicole. One of the interns Labs supported joined the team and took over the physical Lab space which helped a lot, it was the perfect place for him to utilize his skill set - the job role matching that Nicole is so talented at. For two years I was working up to 90 hour weeks, kept getting ill, my family and friends were concerned as they hardly got to see me. I was burnt out. With my managers support, I requested to be made a full-time Enterprise Manager with Labs, meaning I would only be working in one role. However, this request got pushed back again and again, leaving me feeling quite desperate that I had a little breakdown one day at work. Enough was enough. I spoke to Nicole who had been having meetings to try and push for me to be made full time on her team, and nothing was being done - we were both fed up. The next day, Nicole quit her job at Ogilvy on the basis that she couldn't lose her team and couldn't put us through the incredible workload either. Now this is a very risky card to play, as it could easily have backfired, but Nicole stated she would stay if I would be made a permanent member of the Lab team with a raise. My hero. Not often do you find a manager who would step into the fire for you.

But that is Nicole, she has a very strong code of ethics - to treat people with respect and kindness, she fights for those whose voices aren't heard.

To me, this sums up what being in Labs was about - being brave enough to say you don't know everything and smart enough to go and find out, then using that knowledge together with a creative idea and sense of purpose to make a change where no one thought there needed to be one.

So, for the next four years, I worked for Ogilvy Labs helping Nicole fight for those voices. It was perfect for me! I have always felt this strong desire to help others, and with Labs I got to do exactly that - with the power of Ogilvy behind us. My favorite part of working for Labs is that in many ways we were a start up within a large well-known organization, and we used our power for good. Together, with some incredible brains at Ogilvy, we were able to persuade brands to be brave and take risks. We highlighted startups who just needed someone to give them a chance. We gave youths who were dazed by the increasing pressure to have the perfect CV and a degree an opportunity to explore their options without being from a 'perfect' background.

Not to say that these weren't happening already, but through Nicole's passion, they became the driving force of Labs - we were the underdogs with a leader who had the ability to spot trends before they became trends. My favorite saying I learnt from Nicole is 'you don't know what you don't know.' To me, this sums up what being in Labs was about - being brave enough to say you don't know everything and smart enough to go and find out, then using that knowledge together with a creative idea and sense of purpose to make a change where no one thought there needed to be one.

Maybe you are lucky enough to have someone like Nicole in your life, that person who not only sees your talent when you don't, but then forces you to realize that you have no business being small -who instead takes your passion and helps you find a place for it.

Nicole knows she is powerful, take her advice and make it work for you. Acknowledge that fire in your belly and change the status quo. Yes, there will be challenges in front of you, but if there wasn't any, someone else would probably already have done it. Find people who share your passion. Make a plan, or just wing it as a starting point... The worst thing you can do is have a meeting about a meeting about it. Don't wait around, you have got to start somewhere... so just fucking do it."

Problem: Finding and keeping talent in a fast-changing world

Solution: Find, hire and nurture curious and entrepreneurial spirits.

13
REGRETTABLY THE LABS HAVE BEEN SHUT DOWN

*I*t started out as just another day at the office. It was the end of July 2016. A beautiful summers day in London.

Then the tsunami hit.

I remember the day very clearly. I was negotiating a pay-rise for Gemma, who was my right-hand woman and strategist in the Labs. A math and science major and a fabulous geeky girl - she was a 25-year- old super star and exactly the talent Ogilvy would need to hold on to, but she hadn't had a pay raise for a long time. My solution was a creative one, which was good for the agency and meant varying her days and all would be fine. Little did I know, the meeting I was walking into would turn out the way it did.

They told me they were closing down the Labs.

It was as if I'd been punched in the stomach and run over by a truck. It was read to me from a script, zero empathy for someone that had been there for almost 17 years. Then again, I wasn't surprised by anything in the agency or corporate world. I knew the kind of people involved. I knew it had always been an uphill battle. My quest for new thinking and value was tough - the desire to be taken seriously inside such an old model of thinking. I most certainly will not blame all of Ogilvy. It is an incredible company, with many great people, across many countries - but on this occasion, it was down to the spreadsheet mentality of London Group CEO, the Finance Director and EMEA Head of HR. No negative or hard feelings, a simple truth that they will need to take responsibility for their actions. They had their own reasons.

It struck me, here we were, our tiny band of disruptive missionaries trying to drag a 200-year-old industry into the 21st century using our bare hands and minds. We should have known it wasn't guaranteed to end well.

The Innovation Lab was my baby, it was my raison d'etre, it was the sum total of my whole career. I had set it up with a blank sheet of paper. So much hope and vision attached. This was one of the worst days of my life. It was also probably, actually, most certainly, the making of *me*.

Back in April that year, Ogilvy's worldwide Executive Director and EMEA Chairman, had warned the agency would: *"Reduce its investment in the UK if the country voted to leave Europe."* It subsequently did.

He said, *"Certainly we would not invest further in our UK business in a non-EU environment. We would have to make investments elsewhere to serve our clients. Not one of our clients has increased their budgets this year which is in part due to the uncertainty in markets."*

To me this was a good reason for innovation and creativity to be brought more into focus and made more mainstream not closed down. They continued to speak about uncertainty. I thought yes - uncertainty - and yes, we must bring greater creativity and innovation.

The EMEA Ogilvy Chairman again said, *"We are dealing with huge global uncertainties, number one of which for us is the EU position. Should we vote to leave, I see huge decline in our business this year as a shop, and I think we will have seen the high point of the creative services industry in London. From then on it will be a slow and maybe more dramatic decline."*

The Drum (a marketing and advertising news channel) quoted the UK chief executive, from an internal memo where she told staff, *"The agency needed to be better and faster at making work."* following the closure of the self-funded research and development offshoot.

I guess that final explanation by the UK CEO will always leave me baffled. Addled by the scattered logic of outdated agency thinking.

I had one very clear thought. WHY?

Let me add some further context that had led up to this. Paul Simons had left several years ago, and Paul O'Donnell had been promoted to London Group Chairman. Most recently promoted again to EMEA Chairman. Mike Walsh had retired and the agency was under enormous pressure to produce new revenue. It had also moved into a major new building. So, unless new revenue could be produced, then costs had to be cut. I had received amazing amount of support from all of them over the years.

For those of you unfamiliar with it, I should also explain how agencies work. A large global advertising agency is a simple idea on top of a massive machine. The agency (ideally) needs large global clients who (typically) need a single minded *"creative"* campaign placed in all its markets. The agency needs to do this without undue overhead and at maximum profitability. That's because to get the assignment in the first place they need to look the part and then they need to recover the enormous costs that go alongside. Buildings and armies of people who run about a fair bit.

Nobody in leadership really wants to disrupt any of that with innovation and difference - with the exception of the creatives and clients for whom that's the whole point. It actually isn't much different than most large organizations.

So, this is where the rubber hits the road. When an agency needs to create revenue or is looking to reduce cost and when there's a new Finance Director and a new CEO in place - what you have is a perfect storm.

For me this had spelled the end.

It was a time where Dave Trott's insight really shone through - *the irresistible force had truly come up against the immovable object.*

Looking back now, I can see how it all stacked up.

To be very fair, there were attempts at establishing a survey as to why Ogilvy should keep the Labs. It was perhaps well intentioned, but nowadays with Brexit and Trump clear in everyone's minds - asking a question like they did (in a perfect storm) is likely to get a surprising and wrong answer.

The intention was probably to prove its worth - which its main audiences could see but ask it of a wider array of people who weren't looking.

Labs impact was to those solving client problems and involving an external and future looking network of influencers and innovators. As it turns out, that's a tiny percentage of people working in a machine built to sell man hours and deliver profit each quarter.

On the other side of the coin, I could see how the account teams might respond. Many of these were the best suited Oxbridge types I've mentioned before, those who couldn't ever be persuaded to engage with the Lab Days and all that fancy disruption and innovation. They had a day job, which was to make sure the client was happy, and they were doing what they needed to be doing to keep the existing business model intact. That was how they were measured on their success and deliverables which was usually financially driven.

This stuff can't be put into a box and distilled into an easy or standard process. It was just too hard. So, when asked if Labs was valuable to them the answer was very likely to be a flat *"no thanks."* And so, it turned out to be that the Labs would be closed.

The Tsunami hit land. There was massive confusion and consternation across the entire industry. John Tylee, wrote in Campaign in August 2016:

"The writing had been looming large on Nicole Yershon's office wall at Ogilvy Group for a long time. So, it was no shattering surprise for the boss of Ogilvy Labs to be told that her operation was being axed, along with herself and her four-strong team. Ever since joining Ogilvy 16 years ago with a brief to drag the group from the analogue into the digital age, she had always been well aware of the precariousness of her position. Not least because, as a research and development specialist and not a revenue generator, she understood the importance of having influential internal advocates and of how any change in the group's bean counters could spell disaster.

It's never easy for anybody working in research and development – and not just those in agencies. Not only are you a disruptor, but the fact that you're a cost center means you're always in the Financial Director's sights."

Ogilvy's decision to dispense with Ogilvy Labs reverberated across many industries, especially those with Innovation or R&D in their job title. Clients especially sat up and took notice. Labs was seen as a pioneer when it launched in 2007 to educate and stimulate innovation at a time when mobile was seen as the next big thing and Facebook was emerging as a communication game changer. Setting up unique, innovative partnerships and bringing the outside world into the organization.

About four years ago, I met Magnus Jern (Chief Innovation Officer at DMI). He did a brilliant job of curating Mobile World Congress for Ogilvy clients and myself. He wrote recently on the topic of why a "Labs" would fail but should/could succeed.

"*Almost every Fortune 500 company opened an Innovation Lab in the last three years. If their purpose is to reinvent business, they are failing. Many of them have shut down Innovation Labs during the same period. And they include Coca-Cola, Unilever, Nordstrom, and Target.*" They fail because the old model remains resistant to the new.

We prided ourselves on staying ahead of these traps but finally the profit and loss on the excel spreadsheet (P&L) won!

Many other Labs have suffered by being too slow in their decision-making processes or simply by not delivering results. They fail by not taking enough risks and only focusing on incremental innovation - not the big disrupters.

They fail by lacking the necessary integration with the core product and service lines of the business. They are not clear on what problems they are trying to solve.

They fail because they turn into trendy money pits without the required buy-in throughout the organization.

Actually, I feel the role of the Lab was not to invent. It was to be aware of what was going on in tech outside the closed world of the company.

The outside world is presented to the company so employees can be made aware, and act as appropriate, to keep the company up to speed.

This helps it be ahead of the game. In the early days of the Labs opening, every single person had a different understanding of what it was and what it should be. I didn't listen to anyone then, otherwise, we would never have moved forward. I took responsibility and made decisions but not via a committee.

For us at Ogilvy, we were working within an overall company culture that didn't buy into the change it required to embrace innovation as a core differentiator. Or actually, in the end, a CEO or Finance Director that didn't understand the new way of working and how to measure that success. Success for them was on a spreadsheet - you were a number in a large organization, not an individual.

We always knew that we would need to be embedded. Our approach to innovation and testing had to be measurable. We had a central hub with a mandate to push innovation - to help the organization become innovative.

During the creation and incredible journey of the Labs my mantra was simple. And now the global lessons of Labs everywhere ring oh so true.

- **Identify and understand the problems that the business can solve so that we are not solving the wrong problem really well.**
- **Change ways of working and processes so that the time-to-market becomes a few months (and not years).**
- **Understand that it's OK to fail, because otherwise no one will test radical ideas.**
- **Prototype, test, test and test again fast to ensure that the cost of failure is minimal and that the big concepts are identified.**
- **Learn, learn, document share and learn, and then learn again.**
- **Set measurable objectives with data-driven innovation.**

Ogilvy Labs and others like us represented a significant step forward from the Mad Men Era. That was a golden age when big agencies had departments devoted to understanding the science of advertising but not innovation.

Today, a number of large agency groups have innovation arms. I am sure every one of them experiencing a similar pain, it is the nature of R&D. It isn't the usual day job. We are laying the road as we go along and to write a PowerPoint to explain it, is actually quite difficult.

Ogilvy presented the closure of Ogilvy Labs as a cost-cutting measure and described it as a victim of its own success. The CEO of Ogilvy & Mather Group UK, claimed that *"Ogilvy Labs helped to successfully embed innovative thinking across the group and within many of its clients."*

I never believed that embedding innovation across the group would be effective or even efficient. I also don't think that innovation should necessarily be everybody's responsibility. There has to be an awareness of innovation - creative people are naturally innovative - but technology and digital change is exponential. You cannot know everything that is happening with technology now. I always say, *"you don't know what you don't know."* With everyone in Ogilvy doing their day jobs, they were not measured by knowing these things, or building these innovative relationships and partnerships or collaborations. They are measured by their day rate, which involves still doing contact reports that are pages long, that no one reads, or being in meetings for hours with a cast of many, and then getting back from the meetings and having to go through at least 150 emails daily. It is seriously difficult to offer value when all the hours are taken up in this manner.

> There has to be an awareness of innovation - creative people are naturally innovative - but technology and digital change is exponential.

Even a super computer would find it hard keeping up with the enormity of what's going on. In any major business there needs to be intelligent filtering going on to understand the outside world. Otherwise it would swamp people.

It's such a big field that R&D has a genuinely important role to edit the vastness and not distract the actual creative process - that's people doing great work on real cases. That's already a full-time job. Tom Sharman, our last Rough Diamond student in the Lab team made the point that Labs are important because of what they represent:

"The problem is big agencies (or any large organization) suck at innovating and need encouragement. An innovation department often looks like a Rolex to the leadership. They think it's not necessarily needed but looks good to clients. While it does look good, applied properly and integrated within the business it becomes hugely valuable for so many more reasons than that."

The demise of the Lab highlighted an overall uncertainty and misunderstanding by leadership about what agency Labs are actually for. This has created a perennial tension. The techies want Labs to be experimental and the business people want them to produce products they can sell to clients. Everyone has a different opinion on what a Lab should be.

Robin Charney (business director, digital and innovation at AAR Group) said in an issue of Campaign Magazine. *"In closing Ogilvy Labs, I think Ogilvy Group is being a bit short-sighted. Clearly there was a budgetary element to its decision, but Ogilvy Labs was very much a pioneer when it launched. It showed Ogilvy to be forward-thinking and open to innovation, while underlining its belief in the future.*

It would be sad to see it going back on that because, during the past 18 months, I've had countless conversations with clients needing help with the changes now happening in their marketplaces at lightning speed. However, agencies still have to figure out how the Labs model is going to evolve."

I walked away from Ogilvy without signing anything or doing the usual financial deal. I needed to leave with the truth and not a made-up story. This was that they closed down the London Labs - plain and simple. They could not say how much innovation was important or spin any other story, as the truth is the truth. The London group CEO and Finance Director obviously didn't think the Innovation Lab was necessary for their clients or they would not have made that decision. I have no animosity. I understand the benefit I gained working there for so long - but I did not and would not support their reasons for closing it down. Not one of them. When companies become so large, they lack the human kindness that goes with making people redundant. My redundancy was read to me from a script without a moment of empathy or kindness. Perhaps this was doing it by the book, just in case they get taken to court. It wasn't pleasant after almost 17 years there. There becomes no logic, no rationale, and no integrity how they had done it. Sad times for most people in those situations.

In the end, I have set up my own company. Another business entirely and one built on the same open truths as I had always worked with and built trust in all my life. Signing up to an Ogilvy announcement was not the truth is not in my nature - it's just not who I am. I said I'll leave with nothing but statutory pay for almost 17 years' service and I did. No hard feelings. Leaving with the truth meant it was far easier to sleep at night. It means that you are totally in control of your life.

I had amazing global learning lessons from my time there. I just had to look at the benefit and move on. I don't blame Ogilvy the business or the majority of great people who work there. I think it's the same in any large corporate structure, whether it's a bank or anything else. Once a cold financial decision is made you will get frog marched out with just your things in a box.

Eventually, you get over these things. It happens to everyone, it's called life. There's a benefit in it every time that you just need to identify and then deal with. Of course, you go through the pain initially - then you start to come through it.

Soon you are better for it.

I had turned down the money and walked out with the truth. The truth was that they weren't ready to pay for something whose benefits were long-term and couldn't be reduced to a line item with correlated quarterly returns.

The truth was, they would rather quash the only authentically innovative thing they had going for them than risk the unknowns that came with the work that I do.

I wasn't going to malign the character or disparage Ogilvy, but I was going to tell the truth about what happened, because it matters.

I harnessed the power of technology. I lined up my own PR. I reached out to Campaign USA. I wanted the story to be global, not just a London agency making their Labs lady redundant.

I reached out to my network of hundreds of thousands of people. I posted on LinkedIn and Twitter. I was careful with messaging. It wasn't about me. Who cared about one woman and her job? This was a story about a large agency suffering from institutional inertia to the point where it couldn't comprehend the entrepreneurial spirit of innovation that it would need to stay in touch with its clients.

This was a story about a large agency suffering from institutional inertia to the point where it couldn't comprehend the entrepreneurial spirit of innovation that it would need to stay in touch with its clients.

The Labs work at Ogilvy was always longer term than the executives could understand. Any time a business does something purely based on the money, it's probably making a short-term decision not a long-term one.

I was gone.

How Did I Maintain That Gracious Behavior? By "Channeling Alicia"

Transparency and graciousness were under fire. That seemed to be the path and I called up my alter ego to guide me along it.

If ever I felt like I was going to boil over, all I had to do was think about one of my favorite characters - Alicia Florrick, the badass attorney on The Good Wife. She allowed me to engage with my adult self.

In the show, Alicia has to go back to work after a she finds her husband messing around. She wound up well and truly divorced. She had two kids and a career to maintain. She handled herself with grace through terrible circumstances.

I channeled Alicia during difficult times. There would be no lawyers and no drawn-out custody battles. I'm proud of my honesty and my transparency because they allowed me to walk with my head held high.

If it wasn't for my divorce, I think my separation from Ogilvy would have gone quite differently. I just wouldn't have been quite so prepared. But I had recently enough experienced the power of radical transparency. I approached the situation with the same idea.

Again, I channeled Alicia!

I started to emerge with Alicia's help. I became Nicole. Not a cog in a large agency. I had been ripped unceremoniously from my world. One I had built from nothing to something a global agency had become famous for. I was now on my own and in so many ways on my own. It was time to really be myself.

Nicole Yershon

There's danger in having a personal brand. In lots of ways it has become a 21st century shorthand for a strong, clear sense of self.

The downside is a potential for isolation within a large organization and the reality of unproductive dynamics around power. Feeling like they are telling you that you blow your own trumpet. It has always been about the truth. If I or the Labs have had a part to play with an innovative project, then we will shout about it. Before the story becomes changed to suit someone else's agenda.

The truth is the truth - it's always easy to remember and then back up. You have nothing to lose.

The upside is one of transparency and truth. Radical transparency.

By being that clear I could sharpen my principles and build the solid foundation for a new way of working outside the politics of a large global financial machine; these were my guiding principles.

- A Transparency that allows for speed and agility.
- A Transparency that could cut through the inevitable bullshit.
- Transparency doesn't need endless meetings because everything is already perfectly clear.

It was the same transparency that allowed me to walk with my head held high after my marriage broke down and my life changing experience with Ogilvy.

All I wanted was to let my inner child loose. I wanted to scream, shout, hire lawyers, and fight tooth and nail at the injustice. Ultimately, that wouldn't have been good for me.

By *"channeling Alicia"* I would be acting with grace and dignity. It meant I was able to move from Nicole at Ogilvy to Nicole at Nicole. I could finally grow into myself. I could do it fully as a real person.

And that would be me. I'm incredibly grateful for it now. Ogilvy and its actions didn't just let me go. It was as though they fired me out of a cannon with a renewed mission into uncharted territory.

Problem: You lose your job.

Solution: Turn disruption into advantage

14
INTRAPRENEUR BECOMES ENTREPRENEUR

Whack

Freedom was a Heady Cocktail of Emotions - Freedom was a Shock

A new start evoked so many things in me. A big void. The chance to do something new. A lot of new thinking to do. It was exhilarating. It was numbing. I could fly or I could sink like a stone. I could do anything. I could do nothing. I could be caught in the headlights and not know what to do at all.

I had witnessed and survived a fierce storm. In a few short days my whole life passed in front of me. I wasn't defeated. I was alive. I had witnessed all the worst of corporate politics - incompetence, weakness and stupidity. I looked internally and found some peace within my own beliefs. I felt anger, determination and renewal all at the same time.

All these things would hit me without warning and at any moment - at the same time - and in any combination. They did. The hardest thing was to tell my Mum, Dad and my children. I had recently purchased our home from their father. I remember feeling really empowered that when the divorce happened, I was able to buy the family home which meant I didn't need to move them or sell the house. And me, a woman, on her own, totally independent, was able to provide a continued stable environment. Now without a full-time job, what would happen to the mortgage renegotiations and the roof over our heads?

After A Short While These Thoughts Subsided

Being on my own was electric and strange. It is a powerful experience in so many ways. Given how traumatic and extreme recent events had been, I was both cautious and yet always somehow confident.

My incredible parents, children and friends were absolutely amazing. Wow. They gave me incredible strength.

Confidence, at this time was increasingly important to me. Confidence was now driving my every move. I could feel that my learning up until this point had given me something I could really rely on. I didn't need somebody to tell me what to do or when to do it. I didn't ask, *"can I?"* or *"should I?"* I would challenge myself with *"why the hell not?"* I was confident enough not to make excuses. For some reason, I felt calm and that I knew everything would ultimately be OK - but it would be a bumpy road. It's just how life is - with its ups and downs, twists and turns.

I've never needed to be constantly praised. My success has never been dependent on other people's approval. I firmly believed I was completely in control of my own life. I knew I wasn't going to give up the first time something would go wrong, and I could see that problems and failures were merely obstacles to overcome and never a barrier to success. *"What's the worst that can happen?"* was always my motto. Now I had the perfect springboard. I was free.

I've never been one to put things off. I've never been afraid to get cracking. I've always been full on when it comes to change. I've always been confident enough not to put things off. My confidence meant I didn't need to seek attention. And being myself was always more effective than being important.

During my first few days and weeks of freedom, I began to realize just how many important lessons had hardened the diamond in me.

Believe in yourself. Believe that no matter how many people say no, you can trust your intuition and your instincts. It's so easy, especially as a woman, to think "*maybe I don't know, maybe I'm wrong,*" but you've got to trust your instincts and you only trust them if you can develop a strong sense of self. That means knowing your strengths and capabilities.

I've always understood that life isn't perfect. I try to teach all those around me, as well as my kids, that you learn from your mistakes. It's OK to mess up. I'm a massive fan of the real world. It's a messy, unknowable and crazy concoction; the minute you think you know it, you are dead.

Talking Of Crazy Concoctions

During this time, there was a fortuitous and serendipitous meeting in a hot tub in international waters off of Miami. With no connectivity - no mobile phones. I met Jesse Krieger, the amazing publisher who brought about this book.

I remember the first time I went to the Summit at Sea Series - a gathering of 3,000 invitation only, brightest people in business and culture for a voyage across international waters. Their mission was to build community and places that catalyze entrepreneurship, creative achievement and global change to make a more joyful world. I could only afford the package that was referred to as "bunks." They have four people - complete strangers in a tiny cabin. I got as far as the door, looked into the room, and said, "*yeah, right, this isn't happening. It's like sleeping in a coffin, far too claustrophobic for me.*" I'd met this hugely talented chap called Zach the day before. He was supposed to be sharing with another guy, but the guy didn't

want to share a double bed with a stranger, so I stayed with Zach.

I got a double room with a balcony for the price of a bunk! Sounds strange right? But it was all above board, even if it was below deck.

My second time at Summit at Sea, Ogilvy had already paid for my place and my bed. But I wasn't sure I could go, as the Labs had recently been closed down. I didn't have a job, let alone a flight. Serendipity strikes.

Right at that moment, the Advertising Research Foundation got in touch via LinkedIn, which, I may add is incredible with the ability to stay in touch with everyone that I've met over the years. They wanted to set up something for their members around the word "*innovation.*" They were interested to understand why people talk the talk but don't walk the walk. They wanted to offer courses for their members and offer more value.

They had heard that the Lab had closed. It fitted their view about the industries very short term thinking and wanted me to present to their members event in Palo Alto's Facebook office how to innovate in large organizations.

Although they didn't pay speaker's fees, they would fly in their international speakers, so (naturally enough) I combined the two trips.

I could fly from London to Miami and do the Summit At Sea - and hence this book. Then I could fly from the Summit to San Francisco.

There was no cost, but there was a will and from that there was a way.

Most people find the idea of seeking out these events as too hard, too hectic, and all a bit random - dotted about and unconnected. In fact, it's quite the opposite. This is the whole point of creativity and the source of the alchemy. The new ideas and the connections I cultivate are the whole point. Identifying the new thoughts and further connections spark yet more ideas.

I've proven this to myself enough times. Whether at Hatch in Montana or Summit at Sea, wherever innovation is happening the basic idea is to grow my network and the result is an expansion of my thoughts as to what is possible.

Do It

As Dave Trott said, *"the world has plenty of thinkers but a really serious lack of doers"*. Now I've stepped outside the corporate system and enterprise mindset, it's very clear to me that *"doing stuff"* is the precise moment of breakdown.

It's at the very point when corporations cease to adapt, change, and grow. Doing is confused by attending meetings, usually with a cast of thousands. There's endless innovation workshops and planning meetings and great new ideas emerge, but they often don't go anywhere.

People in business seem to not know how to make things happen. It's so prevalent that we can now see a very well-trodden path.

Here's A Scenario To Bring This To Life

Imagine a bright young millennial entering her professional life at a big organization. Because of the stifling corporate culture, she finds herself in, she can neither conform to how things are done, nor can she rally all her strength and go against the grain with an idea that would challenge popular convention.

This would be risking her livelihood. She would be putting her job and her reputation on the line for the sake of innovation. If she is a real creative, someone for whom innovation is her passion and her purpose, she may well find that she cannot fulfill her goals in the corporate environment.

In that case, she sets off on her own as an entrepreneur. This means leaving that corporate culture once again devoid of the creative spirit it so desperately needs. Corporate culture desperately needs this diversity and fresh thinking if it's to succeed in this world.

And A Case In Point - Gemma Milne's Story

I met Nicole on day three of working at Ogilvy. I was one of the selected Ogilvy Fellows - graduates all from top unis, with "high achiever" backgrounds, ready and keen to be welcomed into the world of advertising.

We had three days of training before we started our placements and through this, each of the Ogilvy companies and specialist teams presented what they did. Nicole presented Labs - and I remember her telling us about the Rough Diamond scheme and how amazing people who hadn't been to university were. Obviously that didn't go down massively well with a room full of "high achievers," but something in me must have been intrigued as I emailed Nicole straight after the meeting asking if I could work with her.

She replied saying along the lines of "come get involved whenever" - which to her literally meant "come get involved whenever," but to someone who - at the time was used to big corporates (I was previously at J.P. Morgan), and following rules, and long meetings, and a distinct lack of randomness - it meant "thanks for your interest but who knows how we'll actually work together so never mind."

I worked in account management for a year and a half after the grand scheme and ended up finding it really wasn't for me. I had another go at getting in with Nicole when she was organizing the Internet Of Things Lab day as I was coming up to a year on Amex. As a route to find some contacts, new ideas and frankly, a new job, she welcomed me onto the team. I remember when we were deciding on the name for the conference, we were googling thesaurus results for "connect" for some inspiration.

Nicole was listing words like "attach," "associate," "join" and when she got to words such as "disjoin," "divide" and "sever" I piped up that she had moved from synonym to antonym. In front of the whole team, during our first meeting together where no one really knew each other, Nicole stared at me and said, "You are SO intelligent Gemma." I remember feeling both ridiculously flattered and totally uncomfortable - and this is something that Nicole is very good at doing. She will openly tell you what she thinks of you and big you up, no matter how strange that might feel to other people. She doesn't care about tiptoeing around things, even if it means things maybe get misconstrued.

I feel like "translation" is a bit of a trend with Nicole and I. It took me some time to learn it of course, but in the end - ironically - I ended up being her translator, instead of lost in translation. Nicole always says that I "speak Russian" in the sense that I could translate what was in her mind out into Ogilvy-speak, or whatever other language was needed to get the right point across.

After the Lab Day, I joined the Lab team when a position opened up. Nicole randomly texted me on a Sunday afternoon and asked to meet the next day to offer me the position. It was the most unconventionally awesome way of getting a job. I was used to a four-stage interview processes and official online contact through HR websites. Nicole just said she knew I was right for the role and that I wanted to move jobs so to her it made total sense.

I had been offered another position at Ogilvy at the same time, and while I was deciding, I spoke to the person who at the time was heading up account management - my boss's boss. She told me that she felt the Labs job was right for me as a person but warned me that it might not be good for "career planning purposes." The minute she said that, I knew the Labs job was the right move. I knew working with Nicole, someone who trusted me more than I trust myself, was going to be the best move in my career (and luckily my hunch was right). I knew that career planning wasn't about titles but rather the people you are surrounded with and the freedom you have to grow.

Day nine in the new job and I was flown off to Dubai to stand in front of a crowd of 500 and present my first keynote. Nicole just said I should do it. She told me she didn't need to check my slides as she trusted me. This was the start of a totally new career in which I was working alongside someone as opposed to for them, where I was given so much responsibility and autonomy but also the most support. It was where I learnt that if I didn't just go and do it, it wouldn't get done (the beauty of small, nimble teams operating outside the company remit). I didn't just magically get used to that way of working. Sometimes I struggled with the randomness and the "just do it" - "less strategy" mindset, but it was by far the biggest progression I've had in my career and life and I now can't understand why more people don't work like that.

I'm now the sort of person who hears "no" and thinks "find a way make a way" (my favorite "Nicole phrase"). When wanting to connect with someone, I have no problem randomly approaching them, tweeting them or adding them on LinkedIn. When working on a project, I only focus on the next step and not the enormity of the whole thing, as Nicole always encouraged. All of these things I learnt from Nicole. I know this as people always ask me how I do things and I realize that it wasn't originally natural to me. These were learned behaviors that frankly anyone can do.

Only, of course, if they are privileged enough to have a boss, colleague, mentor and - ultimately - friend, like I do in Nicole.

Connections Are Valuable - Connecting Things Is An Art, But Accountants Are Not Able To Measure It On A Spreadsheet

On August 25, 2011 Steve Jobs famously made the following comment - *"You can't connect the dots looking forward; you can only connect them looking backwards. So you have to trust that the dots will somehow connect in your future. You have to trust in something – your gut, destiny, life, karma, whatever."*

Some may say that making connections - connecting these dots is what makes life so enjoyable and valuable. Making connections certainly seems that natural to me.

Connecting dots, the people, the challenge and the great ideas, is the biggest part of what drives me. I believe that this is what makes innovation and innovation is the raw material and source of all progress. The world needs ideas. It needs them if we are to solve the immense challenges we have. Innovation is what will deal with the inevitable complexity of this new world. It is life and luckily the ability to spot the connections has always fired me up.

Making connections multiplies the chances of value being created. Adding one thing to another thing to make an even better thing. Spotting these connections requires many things but at least a good understanding of the parties concerned. And making different and unusual connections are right at the heart of creativity.

Whether you're an artist, architect, designer, or a software developer, connections empower you. If you are a business leader, politician or change maker powerful connections sit front and central.

Incredible connections are made possible by new tools and technologies that are only just becoming available. We can connect with the world. It's only our mindset that can get in the way of reaching out and connecting. If there's a will there's a way. You can connect with anyone anywhere with just a few clicks and something valuable to say.

I can't think of a role where making the right connections isn't hugely important. Throughout my journey and the essence of the Black Book, connections have been one of the core pillars of success. In my world, connectivity has to be far more than followers or names on a list. My passion is to understand everyone I meet and understand who they know and what they are doing. My mentality immediately engages with other connections and bingo I can start to see something that didn't exist moments ago; a solution to something or an idea that between us we could turn to someone's advantage.

If you aim to survive in the front line of innovation and disruption you had better be sharp on the skill of connectivity.

Technology, that great dispassionate leveler of the playing field, has the power to destroy you if you don't harness it to your advantage. It's a simple fact that if we aren't using it to connect or increase performance then our competitors are. Not being in the driver's seat of your own technological presence can spell the end.

A single journalist or social media writer has the power to destroy your career. But technology also gives you the power to build your own brand.

In my early career, I always viewed myself as an extension of the company I was loyal to and working with. I was always Nicole at GGT or Ogilvy - latterly I was Nicole at Labs.

It was who I was. When it all ended, initially I was seriously uncomfortable. I hadn't just lost my job, I had also lost my identity. I was so wrapped up in advancing the place where I worked that I didn't take the time to really advance myself. Since then, I've been able to build a personal brand around me and all the lessons I have learned.

I'm very happy with being Nicole at Nicole Yershon. In many ways far more powerful. There's no agenda of feeding an advertising agency. I can bring value in its own right. I am able to be myself and not role play. I'm also able to stay transparent and be totally agnostic to the people I am using or bringing in to solve the right problems.

I love working independently. I'm unleashed from any specific business venture. I'm able to have a meeting with someone and make some magic happen just from connecting the dots of previous meetings or encounters. There are not endless meetings with endless committees to agree disagree.

I argue that there's value in personal branding regardless of whether you're inside an organization or out on your own. If you're an entrepreneur, the value of a clear brand is obvious. A brand can help you be distinctive and explain precisely what you stand for.

I have a phrase that exemplifies me *"Innovate – Connect – Disrupt - Inspire."* It makes what I stand for and what I am about very clear. But, even for those who are doing innovative work inside large organizations, I encourage you to develop a personal identity of which your job title is merely a part.

It's good for you and it's good for your company. An enlightened organization will know that it benefits from having motivated and proud people. This attitude promotes everyone to believe and value themselves. It brings about a talent base, one that can stand on its own two feet and make its way in the world by harnessing the contributions of more independently minded people.

Putting It Into Practice

Over the years I've effectively created a template and a framework for innovation. Although it was devised and defined in the advertising industry it's universally applicable. It boils down to a few core truths.

- Be curious and interested in what's going on in the world - not just on your own safe square mile but out there in the real world.
- Be unafraid to do something you've never done before.
- Do stuff - make, execute and ship a product.
- Learn what doesn't work as much as what does.
- Understand the new models and ways that business can work in this digital age.
- Be truthful - even if that means upsetting a few apple carts.
- Be authentic about relationships and fully understanding all the people around you.
- Harvest and constantly refine the network of connections that we all experience in business.
- Recognize diversity and creativity - regardless of job title and gender, race or religion.
- Get buy-in. And that's a result of respect fostered by treating people the way you want to be treated. Motivated and respected people will be there for you and be willing helpers in getting stuff done.
- Be human - not everything is about money. We have a responsibility to go way beyond revenue and profit and do as much as we can for those less fortunate for us.

Now I'm in the real world I can see (far more clearly) how powerful all these lessons were. I've been able to build all this into a really powerful new model for innovation.

Built through connection, embracing disruption, designed with accountability in mind, based on transparency and deployed to deliver results.

I'm now on a whole new path, consulting with small brand agencies, innovation agencies, large media agencies like Havas and clients/brands directly - like Unilever and Tesco innovation workshops. Small start ups that are now looking to scale and needing help to think and work appropriately for this new age.

And by way of example - in 2017 I've assisted with curating and working closely with the founders of a big VR show in London which will continue the "Lab Day" theme. It's designed for 10,000 people to attend, covering VR across medical, defense, sport, fashion, education, entertainment and of course brands.

Outside Of The Comfort Zone?

No, my comfort zone is to be uncomfortable. Uncomfortable with the mundane and the wrong. Uncomfortable with complacency, compromise and ignorance. What use is a comfort zone in a world where everything changes every day and uncertainty is the order of things?

My observation is that comfort is the problem. It's what keeps us stuck with processes and systems that no longer work. Children consistently ask *"why"* or *"how come"* or *"what if"*. They are curious to understand and perhaps know of another way. That's what the disruptors do - they ask WHY or rather WHY NOT. Now that I'm an independent and instead of trying to create change within an existing agency - the shackles are off. I have the ability to try new things.

The biggest challenge now is getting the leaders to accept that they don't need the big logo and all the crazy traditional process to get things done. They should know by now that they can spend millions on a big logo to create change, only to find they've spent millions and are in exactly the same place.

The trouble is they want to innovate, but they're still tied to the traditional employment model.

I met with a client for two hours and within the first two hours, we had pulled together four or five concrete ways to grow the business.

They're working on new technologies with a global player and they need to tell their story in a different way. I explained that this is perfect for virtual reality. I suggested they do an augmented reality overlay on top of a gymnast's routine. The audience would immediately be able to tell if the gymnast was perfectly in form, or how exactly they were off.

At the same time, I could connect them with the right people to move this idea and the business forward, all in the space of two hours. I would check back in a month, see how it goes and move the ball forward again for the next month.

Rough Diamonds thrive in the doing, for it is the doing that polishes our character and lets us truly shine. Rough Diamonds turn disruption into advantage in business and life.

Problem: Not knowing how to run a business by yourself.

Solution: Feel the fear and crack on.

15

LIFE - THE BIGGEST DISRUPTION

The Learning Of Life

*T*he book wouldn't be complete without the backstory. That's what people would typically call *"real life."* The story of my family

and me since my teens. In particular, it is also the story of learning through upheaval. The one that happened abruptly and changed my life so much over the last six and a half years.

Not surprisingly the word that echoes through this book - *"disruption"* also characterized that period.

People talk about the word disruption as something that happens in business. I'm talking about disruption in life. As I have said earlier in this book, I have not seen a meaningful distinction between life and work. To me it has all been so intertwined.

The lessons I have learnt through both life and work have made me what I am. They are interchangeable. They each add value and experience to the other.

I want to use this chapter to explain them and the big impact they had. They informed how I approached work and ultimately how that improved my life overall. You have to fight through the bad to earn the best days of your life.

Growing Up - Growing Through

Growing up was not a struggle. I was deeply privileged compared to so many. I know that clearly now but even then, I always felt I lived a good life. I did not take it for granted and my parents made sure I understood what good values were and how to be properly grateful. It was a good world and I was lucky.

It was a happy time. We lived in the same home until I was 18. My Mum, my Dad, my elder brother Dean, we were only 18 months apart. It was not complicated. Aside from a bit of a disruptive nature, meant that school with their rules and regulations was not that enjoyable for me. As you can imagine, after ready the majority of the book, it is no surprise that I disliked being micro managed. Every step of the way went against the grain. My parents ended up sending me to an amazing finishing school in Hampstead, London, for *"nice young ladies."* It was full of fabulous bohemian girls, many who were diplomats' daughters. They understood travel and there being a bigger world out there with so much living and adventure.

I have wonderful memories of these years. There was never much of anything to complain or worry about.

Eventually, it was time to get my first foot on the ladder of work. My parents had a very strong work ethic even though they were by now well off. They were self-made and they intended me to be too. They suggested work ideas and made them happen for me. I had countless weekend jobs to get my own pocket money. It was the same for my brother, who still has an amazing work ethic, setting up a cleaning business from a blank sheet of paper and making a success of it from total will power. Sink or swim. I have huge respect for him, his values his kindness, his love for Daniel and Mila, my wonderful nephew and niece.

I worked in Petticoat Lane a world-famous Sunday market in East London selling mostly clothes. Getting up at 5:30 in the morning to work in the freezing cold was a total shock to a 13-year-old. But I was a grafter.

I've never done a CV in my life. Things just clicked and stuff seemed to happen for me. The only disruption was when I first started work. That was easy to contrast with an idyllic, actually calm home life, again, aside from a few teenage angst moments along the way.

Looking back now I can easily see I did not have the tools I would need to break into the even harsher world outside of all of this.

The tools I needed were surprising.

Back then I would not even have had the right words for them. One of the biggest turned out to be empathy. Empathy for me meant that I could genuinely understand and feel what others felt. Feeling the pain or sensitivity of others had somehow passed me by.

I had somehow missed how to understand how somebody else was feeling. I later learnt that if you have not experienced any trauma on your own journey, then it's really difficult to understand what someone else is going through. Sure, you can be sad for them, and that must not be confused for caring, but you cannot really feel it in in your heart and your soul, which is where you need to feel it. That is what will make you truly human.

As I mentioned before, we talk about disruption in business but really, it's how we put it into our whole life that matters and makes the difference.

Once there's a big shift in our lives and we are forced to deal with it we get disrupted in every way possible. It invades every aspect of how we think and behave - it alters how we show up and how we deal with others.

It is how we choose to learn from it and become better not more damaged people that marks us out.

Mastering it means we can better operate as disruptors, adding value far more broadly within a working environment.

I want to take you on a journey - one that threw me into a period of true destruction and the learning that gave me. It was a journey of experience on top of experience. How I faced up to it and how that made me better in my work. It explains how I became a better person through understanding what makes people tick.

I can see it with hindsight. It required a high degree of emotional intelligence - being aware of myself and the values I had as well as the ones I did not. It became more important to me to have a better developed EI (Emotional Intelligence) than IQ.

EI is our ability to use emotional information (from yourself and others) to better inform how we behave. Being self-aware and able to empathize are the two skills that enable us to do this. I read this recently:

"It's proven that those with a high EI are highly in-tune with those around them. Consequently, they are better able to communicate, build meaningful relationships and so are powerfully able to influence and inspire."

I married my childhood sweetheart. We did marry young, in my early 20's. We had two kids, Claudia and Max pretty much one after the other. I fell pregnant immediately with both of them. I never had any difficulties falling pregnant.

I also did not have the hassle my friends had with boys. My friends had the rejections and entire catalogues of disastrous relationships. That all just passed me by.

I knew I had had a privileged upbringing. My Dad had been hugely successful. My parents were amazing. I only left home when I got married.

My existence was part cotton wool ball and part Truman Show. My salvation was a very strong work ethic. An ethic that was instilled into both me and my brother from a very early age. I was never given anything on a silver platter. We all worked hard for everything that we had.

There I was, married and working at GGT and then Simons Palmer. I was living a very intertwined life with all the whirlwind that goes with that. This book has given you all the detail of what that taught me.

As time went on, life went on too and as we all know, there's nothing we can do, things just change. I found myself separating from my husband. I'm now going through the trauma that a lot of people experience all around the world. The pain and destruction of divorce. It was a very painful time.

I remember some time before all this happened that my best friend Liri Andersson (a visiting professor at INSEAD) was having a bit of a difficult time with a boyfriend. My attitude would always be to solider on and I would say *"come on - onwards and upwards"* or some other well-meant but useless phrase. I didn't really understand the pain that she was actually going through. I would simply think she would inevitably get over it.

And then it happened, thirty years of being together was over. Disruption hit. Onwards and upwards was not going to work for me either. Liri was there for me but she couldn't say to me *"onwards and upwards"* because she knew it was pointless. I'd probably be on the floor in a heap, crying in the fetal position.

I couldn't believe there would ever be any light at the end of the tunnel. I hadn't been prepared for this. I had no tools or equipment. What I did have was a tremendous set of friends and family. It turned out that that was what I needed and would come to value the most too. Friends that are too many to mention. Liri, Sam, Tracy, Nici, Tara, Nat, Caroline, Mark Herman, Dave Erasmus, John Klepper, Yochy, Alex, Karina, Jo, Jo, Kirsty, Kerry, Katz, Sonya, Binki, Alison, Jeanette, Robin, Priya, all my precious HATCHERS and so many others, they will know who they are.

It was my close immediate family that brought me through. My Mum, Rita, and my Dad, Michael were an absolute rock. Along with my brother and my kids, Claudia and Max. They got me to a bigger, better, stronger and different life. I came to realize that to live and move on you can't start the next chapter of your life by rereading the last one.

The Reality Of Divorce #1

It was actually happening that I was splitting from my childhood sweetheart. My first and only thought was for my children. I didn't want them to have to go through what I've seen happens to many other children when parents get divorced. I've also witnessed, through others, the carnage lawyers leave behind. I made the decision that I wouldn't go through lawyers when I got divorced.

I didn't want them to make things even worse because the relationship I wanted to keep secure was for the benefit of the children. I knew my husband and I needed to split in a civilized way. I believed we were adult enough and with me channeling Alicia I would be able to see it through as well as control my rampaging inner child.

However upset I might be there was nothing to be gained by bad mouthing anything or my husband. From somewhere I summoned the strength of character to know that he loved the children as much as I did.

What would be gained by protracted and expensive litigation that lined the pockets of the lawyers. We split everything down the middle.

We took the path of mediation - it was as clean break as you could possibly get given the long-term nature of our relationship.

The capability I drew on most and became the most important throughout this whole thing was given to me by my parents. Be gracious at all times.

"Be pretty if you can, be witty if you must - but be gracious even if it kills you."
- Elsie De Wolfe

Being gracious allowed me to engage my adult self - to be more rational. Never to be emotional never to engage that emotional child inside. Leave that child alone, the child that always creates the tantrum - that screams and shouts.

I focused myself to think about what was important for the long term - the children and their futures. Simple.

Being gracious is hard at first but then it wraps itself like armor around you. It's incredibly powerful when the penny really drops. It makes you ten times stronger. If you're trying to get shit done no matter what - be gracious about it. People will be inspired and help. Being emotional doesn't work. People look away, they disengage, they actively work against you. You can't move forwards.

Being gracious allows you to stay above the fray, it clears your mind and you can be rational about everything. There's no ulterior motive. You just stay in control and keep moving forward, slicing through everything more calmly, quickly and efficiently than everyone else.

Finding Alternative Energy

Both important and another big lesson was when feeling like this you definitely start lacking the energy you need. It's draining.

We tend to keep it inside, so emotion and sadness sucks it out of you. My solution was to surround myself with good people. People of my tribe, people who were happy to give me energy when I didn't have very much.

I've always been able to identify and connect with these people. You know they are the rocks and you see their value increase as you look back and that's all possible because they are all continuously looking forward. I needed reminding of that sometimes.

Once again it was my Dad that taught me this, he said, *"Unless you are moving forward then you're going backwards."*

Just When I Thought It Was Safe

As time passes, and like millions of others, I'm getting over the trauma that was my marriage breakdown.

Another enormous shock and one that hit the whole family hard. Mum was diagnosed with a serious form of cancer. Living each day with knowledge like that and especially when you are a fixer is hard. You're used to fixing things. With this particular thing you start to realize this maybe something you can't fix.

I am together with the family running about and trying everything. Every which way - try this - try that. Everyone that could be spoken was spoken to. Dots that could be connected were connected and dots that didn't yet exist were brought to bear. We got fully onto the case.

Mum was an utter inspiration to me. It was another moment in my life when I appreciated the upbringing and the love they had showed me. It reminded me of their shaping of me. A job that they had done with love and other qualities - much of which I probably hadn't even yet appreciated.

When the diagnosis was made, they were both incredibly pragmatic and practical. Their first thought was to make sure they made myself, my brother and the wider family feel better. They knew and they needed us to know that they had had the most incredible life together.

They wanted us to know that they did everything with zero regrets. They were just going to figure this out and cope with it as needed and in a positive manner.

For my part, it gave me the resolve to not be a victim of why this happened to me. They made me accept fully that it's just life. It happens to everyone. We live, we die, repeat.

This shock reminded me that there are ways in which you can control your own brain to think the right things. You can tell your brain to kill the bad or unhelpful thoughts. After some time, you can train the muscle of your brain. Eventually you can control most, if not all your emotions. You can choose how you're going to deal with things. So, after the shock, and very early into the whole proceeding, I was positive. I've got this.

Waves Crashing

I was very good at compartmentalizing. I noticed that out of all the females I knew I could do it better than anyone. It was how I could dispassionately manage and oversee so many projects at the same time.

Subconsciously though I was living with it every single day. Now on top of the divorce there was my Mum going through chemotherapy and being super brave.

I was beginning to realize that I was human after all - not a robot. No matter how hard I tried it was permeating my brain. From the minute I woke up to when I closed my eyes at night.

These thoughts were permanently at the forefront of my mind. It was proving especially difficult to live through life with the knowledge of someone who you love greatly is living with a serious illness.

Initially she was given three months to live if she didn't have chemotherapy. She went the route and did it every two weeks for two years. Although we lived with it continually, we celebrated absolutely everything. We would get together for dinners - all of us - the whole time - for every occasion. Everything was a celebration.

Moving. Just Moving

There's a great Martin Luther King quote that summed things up for me - *"If you can't fly then run - if you can't run then walk - if you can't walk then crawl - but whatever you do you have to keep moving forwards."*

I can't just stand still.

Life is disruption and disruption was my life. I came to realize this with a vengeance through these years. What I had now witnessed in my personal life was what I had been managing at work. The two became intermingled now and while it was a lot to process, I could still see how valuable the lessons were.

You can't be frightened of things happening like this. You quickly realize that you just have to go with it. Yes, it's like riding a rollercoaster – there will be highs and lows. I was getting as used as possible to living with my Mum's diagnosis, but it was ever present. I had to deal with it. But some days it was just too dark – overtaking pretty much everything that was going on in my head. I knew I needed to get some kind of control back.

A friend of mine named Gal Stiglitz ran a course called *I Discover 360*. He said to come and do the course. He thought it would help me come to terms with everything that was happening and the feelings that I had and couldn't get sorted in my mind.

It was a real turning point for me. It allowed me to understand a major part of my emotional makeup and the parts of my psyche that may have simply been missing. It allowed me to see my Mum for who she was. It allowed me to see that anything that I might have seen as a negative was actually a benefit to me.

It allowed me to brush the unimportant things off my shoulders. I had never really realized these things as values until I did the course. I had not seen quite what an influence my Mum had been in my career.

My Mum was alive, and these insights allowed me to spend the time to let her know that I understood and respected what she had given me.

Getting in touch with myself in this way had many brilliant side effects.

Back in the day I would phone up to discuss something work wise. I would say, *"Oh Mum, can you please put Dad on the phone?"* Now I had changed my behavior and would say, *"Oh Mum, what do you think about this?"* We could now engage in the conversation.

The course allowed me to think straight. I couldn't cope with not being able to think straight. I worked on myself and I could know myself that much better. I got to a renewed state of clarity.

Knowing my brain better meant feeling better. It helped me to move through things much more quickly and efficiently. This degree of clarity allowed me to get stuff done again. It enabled me to just do it, whatever it was.

There's no compromise and there are no regrets. Just doing it gets everyone moving then we can start to test and learn. I don't ever see failure. I just see something not working as initially anticipated as learning. That works for me as a person and I never pass judgement on anyone.

The two years watching my Mum suffer through cancer was a tremendous lesson in coping with adversity. At the time it was hard to see positive things in the whole experience, but in retrospect I see that the strength I gained in that crucible.

Divorce #2

Redundancy at the agency was a major event. But I had faced adversity before. I'd spent my career at the agency doing things that had never been done. I was used to flying without the safety net. Leaving was as hard a blow as ending my marriage.

I'd been with my husband for thirty years, I simply couldn't imagine life without him. Likewise, I couldn't imagine life without being in a big brand agency. I was synonymous with that brand.

I Truly Felt Like My World Had Ended

After a while, and as I looked around, everyone was just going about their days as though nothing had changed. And it hadn't – certainly not for them. After those first few shell-shocked days, I too could look a little deeper.

I saw that all these people had their own pain, their own loss. Quite probably they too were walking around shell-shocked wondering how everyone else looked so composed.

Soon enough, the adversity of that tumultuous time became a source of strength. If I could get through all that, I could get through anything. And that was just as well.

And The Next Crisis

The agency had done its thing. I was more than a little shocked. I had just got a lawyer involved and I was away in Paris with my best friend Liri. I was coming back on the Eurostar and I got a phone call from my brother to say my Dad was in the hospital, he had just suffered a heart attack.

My Dad, Mike Yershon was advertising royalty. Just recently he was named by the IPA in the top 50 game changers in the last 100 years, of the UK Advertising industry.

He worked at the front line of the industry in the days where media was part of agencies (not separated as now). He truly was an original Mad Man. He was at McCann in the late 60's and then Collett Dickenson Pearce (CDP) in the heyday of advertising. He then became a member of the top management of Leo Burnett, UK, as Vice Chairman, responsible for media, research and sales promotion. When he set up on his own in 1980, initially as a strategic media consultant, he took a stand for his beliefs and was also prepared to disrupt. Changes happen all the time and we must never think we live in exclusive or unique times. Things are just different. He saw that the distribution of agency salaries was grossly unfair and inequitable.

How the structure worked at the time would give 27 percent of the money to account handlers, 26 percent to creative and 10 percent to the media guys. When you realize how important the placement of ads is in the market and just how critical and high a percentage of the budget goes towards buying the right space and channel makes you question the mentality of the entire industry.

The attitude in those days also meant that *"media"* and *"placement"* got the last slot and the least time in the client meetings or pitches.

My Dad was one of a small group of visionaries who took the art of media out of full service agencies and created media independents.

Now looking back, we have a good laugh about this. When I was first in advertising everyone used to say, (when people heard my surname) *"Are you any relation to Mike?"*. He was in Campaign every week . Now they say to him, *"Are you any relation to Nicole?"* As you can imagine the journey back from Paris on Eurostar was an absolute nightmare. Thoughts and panic racing through my head. I was unable to stop the images and feelings from making me fear the worst.

My brother picked me up from the station and we went directly to the hospital. Thank goodness - Dad was fighting fit. He had had a stent put in and everything was OK.

The panic was over, the fears subsided. I remember it clearly, we had an interesting conversation at the hospital about the lawyers.

We came to a decision, while Dad was in the hospital on the bed. We even spoke to the lawyer at the same time. We would not be proceeding with lawyers with the agency. I didn't proceed with lawyers with my divorce. I didn't go through 30 years to have lawyers get in the way and make things one hundred times more complicated. We all decided it was best to just cut clear.

We would just understand the benefits that I got, and it was time to move on. I could and would walk with the truth.

Connecting the dots looking backwards shows us that things happen for a reason. My divorce, the agency madness, my mother's and father's health scares, they made me appreciate everything in a whole new light. The light served to deliver me a whole new association with truth.

Dealing With The Truth

Truth has always served me well. Now the brutal truth of what had happened would serve to spare me from negativity. Truth showed me that negativity doesn't deliver you any value at all. All negativity does is drain your batteries and stops you from moving forward.

Truth also gave me the insight into transparency. Transparency is key in most areas of life and you can apply it to yourself. It can allow you to see things clearly and to discover what really drives you. Adversity is a great teacher of brutal truth and transparency.

You have to know yourself and discover who you really are at times like this.

Transparency has changed everything and everyone. Just look at the world we live in today.

Alternative facts, post truth, filter bubbles and echo chambers. Just about every institution we grew up believing were beyond reproach are now busted by scandal, corruption or unfortunate leaks. Transparency happens whether we like it or not. We are easily seen to be what we really are. Fragile, imperfect and human beings.

We need to be always conscious and always on our game. We must always stay seekers of the truth.

The Paradoxical Journey Of Life

Paradox is very revealing about the way we live and explains a lot about our human nature. A paradox is self-contradictory. Typically, it contains two ideas or statements that are both true. But surely, they cannot both be true at the same time?

My journey has been full of them.

The more I knew, the more I knew that I didn't know. The more I saw how brutally hurtful the truth was, the more the hurt would subside.

I've always worked on the basis of knowing and developing my values. Knowing them helps me to know who I am. Developing them stops me from any false sense of arrogance or complacency.

Technology is a great leveler in business, it can improve great processes and make them clear to their audiences. But paradoxically technology exposes the weaknesses too. Nowadays customers have the ability to see straight into the firm. PR cannot paper over the cracks of what isn't there in the first place, like it could back in the day. The eyes of the world are invited in and in they come. They take no prisoners.

I'm actually thankful that there is no room for the smoke and mirrors to create the false gods in industry anymore. My journey made me a seeker of truth. I had had enough of all the bullshit and I was now out to balance the books.

You may be able to spin a story that's not the truth. But eventually you will be found out and exposed. With the march of technology, that exposure today, is sooner than ever before. My journey proved to me that if I was to move through the world the way I needed to me would have to be brutally honest and true to myself.

In a world where mystifying everything and celebrity is supposed to get you everywhere the paradox of brutal truth would become the fundamental pillar of my brand.

My journey took me to Brenne Brown. Her incredible TED Talks point to having open and honest conversations with yourself and others.

She made the incredible observations about needing to show vulnerability. The honesty of that also helped me understand more of who I was, that I was by no means perfect and importantly not alone on this journey. A wonderful paradox - being less vulnerable to anything by being more vulnerable to everything.

Now I encourage and help others going through difficult times to see the worth and value in themselves. I can prove to them (as living evidence) that paradoxically everyone can go through seriously difficult times and be the better for it.

My journey proved to me the importance of keeping things simple. I've never seen behind the reason why people seem determined to complicate things. Why do they do that? It just doesn't help you move forward.

It Was The 26th January 2017 - My Mum Passed Away

6:45 in the morning. Her passing was actually a poetic and beautiful moment. I can't imagine I will ever experience anything quite like it again.

Given the journey I had been on it represented the pinnacle and sum of all my emotions as well as the enormous chasm that it represented. In a wonderful way, my Mum gave the most incredible gift to us all. It was exactly what this is all about. The ultimate paradox.

It's about life - not death.

The end of life is a certainty alongside many other certainties.

It's how you cope with them that makes you.

She passed with all her family around her. It was closure to a lot of the pain and suffering that she had experienced. It was very calm, there were no dramatics and no scenes. It was just beautiful.

It also allowed me to put to bed everything I had been experiencing. But I knew that life wouldn't be the same again. I was really grateful that for the last few years since her diagnosis, I could make myself the best I could be for her.

I was so lucky that I could take that hard look at myself and learn my new way of being. My latest paradox, my new normal of not being prepared to be normal.

A human life is a journey with problems to solve and lessons to learn. We either learn early or we learn late, but we hope to learn eventually. Disruption is the driver of life and a better life is learning to live with disruption. I had learnt that the best life of all was learning to turn the disruption into advantage.

Problem: Loss happens to us all

Solution: Convince your brain to pick yourself up and get on with living

16

WHOOSH!

A year flew past.

*N*ew York City has always been an inspiration to me. I love its audacity. It never ceases to surprise. Whenever I return and wander through its neighbourhoods it's as if it's for the first time.

NYC lifts my spirits. I love its utter resistance to standing still.

New York is a collection of small tight-knit communities—some more tight-knit than others. The City was built through grit, diversity and teamwork. As far as I can tell, nobody ever told the New Yorker that something couldn't be achieved. If they did, they thrived on the challenge.

The buildings are taller, the days are longer, and the determination runs deeper than almost anywhere I've been. You can taste the place.

NYC—The Nicole Yershon Collective.

Soul Sisters.

Publishing the book coincided with me developing my own company and the model behind it. The book took all my learning but gave rise to so much. Writing it, allowed me to define who I am and what I am not. So many people reached out to give me their feedback. People I have never met told me what the book had given to them—that meant so much to me. This was a time when I finally realised that my life journey was all about working out what I didn't want.

Now, a year later, everything I do is summed up in three letters—NYC.

A Tale Of Two Cities

The NYC has a lot in common with New York City.

Like the city—my business is built on the collective efforts of a diverse and passionate bunch of people. It describes the collective intelligence and energy of teams built specifically to get stuff done.

Nothing is impossible with a business model that's designed to expertly leverage unlimited capability. It means that both the resource and the possibility are infinite as long as you can trust them. Trust is essential with our collaborations and partnerships.

Leverage means I have at my disposal whatever is needed to solve a problem or exploit an opportunity. It means I can focus on making sure it's the right problem or opportunity. Harnessing the true power of the gig economy.

Technology allows us to work anywhere. We are truly global citizens with no need to be tied to an office from 9–5.

Unlimited Additions

The first edition of this book was a wild ride.

The Travel—It took me all over the world. It became a #1 Best Seller on Amazon. I did book signings and launches everywherefrom Madrid to Boston, from Los Angeles to Lisbon.

New Friends—I made so many new friends. Bizarrely, I even found time to launch it in my hometown of London. I'm thrilled that it touched so many people and I was able to understand what they took from the book.

The Doubt—Countless times I remember thinking who on earth would want to read this book, but I just kept going. It was a difficult period of time, you've read the book. You know just how difficult. I kept telling myself that at least my Dad would buy the book. My Mum never would. I finished it, I got my story down and that can never be taken away.

Fresh Opportunities—So many people found inspiration in it that I turned one of the central ideas—'intrapreneurship' into a series of online courses. This meant that many more people could turn their ideas into actions. I have now been able to create this new chapter as a new edition comes out.

Itchy Feet

Travelling so much is an addictive drug for the creative soul.

New cultures, fresh thinking, strange languages and different atmospheres. All of it becomes an amazing stimulus for the curious mind. It also proved my business model. I really can be anywhere and still make my business work.

One example of this, among so many during the year was creating an 'inspirational event' in London for 60 people. They came from all over the world. At the same time, our team was scattered all over the world. We took the brief and shaped the whole agenda. We built the team. We managed the curation of the many contributions and experts, we figured out and designed each of the venues. We identified and contracted with the partners. We handled all the logistics and yet the entire experience was planned without ever meeting the client. In fact, the first time we met was as they walked into the experience itself.

As I've mentioned earlier in the book teamwork is an amazing thing to build. In this case, a large number of people, who didn't even know each other before the session, came together to learn and make a better plan for their future.

I'm sure many of them were sceptical coming to the event, but trust was finally formed through the day and they really made progress. This trust was a result of the confidence they could feel. Confidence in the team we put together, in the experts and experiences we curated and confidence in the way the whole day unfolded. They are still talking about that day!

Dave Trott, in my time at GGT, ran the agency like a football/soccer team. He would say that if you're a goalkeeper then stay in goal. Don't even attempt to come out to score goals. Everyone must play to their strengths, rely on the expertise, trust in their teammates and fully understand the role of their position.

A Real Virtuality

The new world arrived for many more people.

A big challenge is how the future of work is going to affect us all. For NYC and its clients, it drives a lot of the work we do. Automation, AI, Machine Learning, culture, the new business models, the technologies, the call for innovation—they are causing the change that demands wholesale transformation.

These days it's possible to run complete campaigns on a global basis armed with just data and competency in the right technologies. This is already a massive part of how things are right now. Examples like this are present in every industry and is at the heart of the disruption we see everywhere.

However, at the very beginning of a complex program of work, there's no substitute for really understanding the requirement, the humans responsible and a clear sense of their aims. All the decision makers need confidence in those working to make it happen. That is often us.

It will be a while yet before the machines inspire the emotions and the integrity to get stuff like this done. In the meantime, our focus remains on developing the relationships that breed getting things done.

Always Learning

Mastering the art of impatience—not really.

Anyone who knows me knows that patience isn't my strongest card. But being open to learning from people I trust and respect really is. I'm working on the patience part, but I came to rely on my *"open to learning"* part this year.

I have learnt so much.In truth, a lot of lessons I've had to re-learn. These were the things I knew *"intellectually"* but they made so much more sense as they smacked me in the face. It mattered more somehow.

Lessons are sometimes hard to learn just through conversation. You hear other people's experiences, they make senseand you agree with them.

Then POW right in front of you, it becomes very real. Brutal sometimes. The most valuable lesson I pay attention to is peoples actions speaking louder than words.

Business 101

My business wasn't going to happen on its own.

I had to figure out how to actually run a business rather than just be a part of one. I learnt the tough way, that rather than business arrive at my door I had to go and knock the doors down myself. Each month a real anxious feeling without a monthly pay-cheque.

My Dad's words rang in my ear a lot this year. Even though I was manic all the time, I always wondered when the next gig would show up. As ever, he was there with the sage advice:

"Don't worry about each month, that's an arbitrary construct and an unwelcome addiction. Just get to the end of the year and then check to see if you've financially survived—more money coming in than going out".

I learnt to be patient and get to the end of the year. It wasn't easy, but I settled into it. I learnt the real meaning of cash flow and accounting in this new world. Things needed to work as the clocks do. People needed to depend on me, and I needed dependable people on my team. I didn't always get it right.

There's Always A Fence

And too many people are sitting on it.

Of course, I had understood the concept, but I hadn't fully appreciated how many people sit on the damn fence. Many people don't firmly commit. Whether it's a meeting for coffee or a contract they need to get done. I also hadn't realised quite how long the fence was. As a result, I found out who really belonged in my tribe. I understood first hand that there are some people who just go that extra yard and that's the yard that matters.

When you're on your own and running the show, you have to go with your gut and create your own luck. You develop a keener sense of where to invest your valuable time because you make much more painful mistakes.

I didn't rely on funding, it has been totally bootstrapped all the way.

The feeling of being an entrepreneur is intense. It's amazing to be fully in control of your own destiny. It's me who is paying the mortgage, putting the food on the table and paying the college fees.

The Advantage Of Disruption

It's been a crazy year all round.

I had to live by my motto—turning disruption into advantage. There is nothing more certain than disruption. There was little that encouraged me more than working with incredible clients. Some of them generous enough to write testimonies to the work of the team. *(You can see these at the NYC website nicoleyershon.com)*

Who knows where the future goes—but it will definitely be disruptive.

Global chaos is there for all to see. It's a very volatile time in every sense. Disruption remains one way to sum it all up. Those of us comfortable with disruption have plenty to do—for those who ignore it then uncertainty and challenges are inevitable.

Those that can translate the disruption, turn that into something of value and make it happen will be the ones that matter in the future.

There are far too many businesses still *"ticking the boxes"* when it comes to their own transformation. To really stand a chance business must embrace new concepts and alter their entire platforms and models—fresh ideas that are powering the decades to come.

It's very hard for businesses to be objective about themselves. There is no way that they can keep up with what's happening outside of their own contexts and preoccupations. In many cases they haven't even got past breaking down the silos that slow them down every day. I continue to focus on bringing the future forward in the right way for each business.

The Integrity Business

This year taught me to rely on one quality in particular.

Integrity.

It's a quality that's often got me into trouble when working for others—being totally honest. For me, it's the first principle of getting anything achieved. It's the definition of integrity.

We all know that making anything meaningful happen in business requires hard work. It takes people who do what they say and people who know what needs doing. We know what happens when people don't do what they say and we feel it much more when they don't know what they're doing.

We have to trade on honesty to get things done. That's where I am right now. I am supremely excited and optimistic about the future. I am even writing another book on the subject.

And Onwards

The year ahead fills me with excitement and expectation - but still there's that tingle. I'm never really sure what's going to come down the track. I guess that's the point really. Nobody can ever be sure and you have to be good with that.

The more you make fixed plans the more they will trip you up. The more you get used to the future being unpredictable the less scared of it you will be. The only thing you can ever do is surround yourself with people that get you and share your attitude.

I think I like the thrill of the cliff edge. It keeps me on my toes and makes me determined to find a way however big the challenge. I would never say it's not daunting nor does it ever make me complacent.

Whatever the future brings I just know that anything is possible.

Problem: This book has come to an end…

Solution: Write another book!

EPILOGUE

*W*ell, here we are again.

The last chapter, this time at the end of the second version of the book and yet another bunch of firsts for me. Why would that be a surprise? Every day should be a first!

Since the book was first launched, I've witness so much more. I've seen my Dad become a kid again and instead of retiring, he has become an unstoppable entrepreneur starting so many new business ideas that an incubator would be ashamed.

At the same time, I've seen my entrepreneurial kids give up normal businesses and strike out on their own and go travel the world. To say that I am proud of them all is the biggest understatement .

My Dad strapped back on his six-shooters and created so much impact in so many unsuspecting fields. My kids decided that they want to live lives on their own terms – without the stupidity of the systems that I am trying to disrupt.

How cool is that?

Basically, it's been an incredible year and the tribe around me stayed true. I survived the onslaught of the post-book launch era and lived to tell the tale. Not without its challenges but the book has been really well received. It has been the reason why I've been asked to speak but most of all, it remains the bedrock of what I do in business and the values I try to bring to life.

No matter what the topic of question, I'm turning disruption into an advantage – and because I'm all about the doing I am focused on identifying the shortest distance possible between disruption and advantage. I call that execution.

Here are this year's top examples of the questions I get:

- How do I get stuff done amongst all the chaos and disruption flying around me?
- How can I get ahead and disrupt the competition instead of being disrupted by it?
- Where do I get the answers I need for my strategic questions in order to survive?
- Where should my business be headed within all this complexity?

But, in all of them, there's one question that surpasses them all -

- How do I get there and leverage the right capabilities with objective and impartial support along the way?

A year on and I'm running a business. My own business. It's actually happening.

I went through so many iterations. It was like being a spinning top inside a whirlpool. Pretty much all of the thinking and figuring it out happening in the background as I worked out the best way to tell my story and make it meaningful. It's quite a challenge because what we do is so different and means different things to whoever I meet. And I meet so many people each of whom has a very different need for the same skills.

I called it The NYC – The Nicole Yershon Collective. Apparently, a city in the USA decided to steal it and use it too. I don't mind.

About The Author

Nicole wouldn't be offended if you said she lacks patience.

She would almost certainly take it as a compliment. The impatience has grown alongside the current climate in society and especially in business. It's quite shocking to think that we are in the 21st Century, with so much incredible possibility, and yet so little critical thinking and action.

Business is (often) designed to stand in the way of what's best. That means the business gets mediocre at best and that mediocre is often too late anyway. That's why Nicole is right impatient to do something about it and that also makes her a maverick and the original Rough Diamond.

A couple of other words in the same breath to describe Nicole – integrity and iron-willed. As has been said many times where most of us say *"why not"*, she will already be halfway through doing it.

She is very hard to pigeon hole, an orchestrator, consultant, mother, speaker, author, judge, mentor and connector.

She defines disruption.

Head to the website at nicoleyershon.com and see a full client list, set of references, skills and how to find out more.

With Great Thanks

This book would not have happened without the contributions of some very special human beings. They were there for me on the journey and weathered the storms with me during the light and the darkest of days. They all played their part. I know I will have forgotten many and I apologise!

My Family:

Rita Yershon, my inspirational Mummy. I started this book when you were physically here in this world, so I had no choice but to make you proud and finish it. I feel your presence each moment of every day and know in my heart how ridiculously proud you would be knowing it now exists

Mike Yershon, my unbelievable rock of a Daddy (aka Pops). Words cannot express the huge, enormous respect I have for you. It's an utter privilege to be *"Mike Yershon's daughter."*

Claudia Salador, my incredible daughter. I love you for putting up with me, for helping me get shit done and always being supportive in spite of the chaos I can cause. Extremely independent, a true friend and now a real partner in crime.,

Max Salador, my wonderful son. I love you for being quietly strong and smart. You are the inspiration for the title of this book. I never stop learning with you and am so proud of the man you are.

Dean Yershon my amazing brother, who I know I can always rely upon. Another entrepreneur, setting up your business with a blank sheet of paper and showing me the way to never give up.

Daniel and Mila Yershon, thank you for always supporting your Auntie Nic.

My Business:

Dave Trott, Caroline Snowsill, Anushka Sharma, Jack Churchill, Kim Arazi, Adah Parris, Amanda Bravo, my wonderful and immediate NYC teammates who have helped and supported me every step of the way. They help make NYC the business it really is.

Chris Rawlinson and Jake Courage for creating my amazing online course. Alison Norrington my storytelling authoress in crime. Nici Phoenix Malamoglou and Tara Austin my muse lionesses.

Jesse Krieger, had we not met in that hot tub at Summit at Sea then this book would never have happened.

Liri Andersson for always being right. Huge respect and love. Tracy Hart, life long friends since we were bumps in our Mummy's tummies. Mark Herman, you are always there, zero judgements and a huge creative talent. Katz Kiely, and all our life's lessons that make us stronger and wiser. Sam Novik, my incredible soul sister. Kerry Marks, we believe in each other always.

My Simons Palmer Girls - Jo Hollis, Jo Friend, Karina Parker and Kirsty Dye. A whole lot of history and an enormous amount of love. Chris Denson, regardless of time zones, thank you for always making me feel like I'm not going mad, that I'm quite normal and to keep going.

John Caswell, you really are my secret weapon. I am full of gratitude with your help every step of the way. *"It is always good"*

THE
NY
COLLECTIVE
TURNING DISRUPTION INTO ADVANTAGE

Turning Disruption Into Advantage

After launching the book, I also turned it into an online course.

It is a tool for helping you learn the art of getting things done. It's a rapid primer helping you move projects forward alongside learning from some of the best creative minds in the industry.

In the interactive course, you will get the chance to challenge yourself together with some of my great mentors and teachers. You will get invaluable lessons on how to become an intrapreneur. You will be able to start to practice your own capacity for innovation.

Lessons you can access anywhere, anytime.

It's an interactive course with video contributions from:

- Rory Sutherland – Executive Creative Director of OgilvyOne
- Dave Trott – President's Award for Lifetime Achievement in Advertising
- And me plus many more…

The Nicole Yershon Collective

As you have read in this book, Nicole is a maverick, inspiration and the original Rough Diamond. She and the team have built The NY Collective (NYC). A modern response to the many needs of business in this tumultuous era.

Nicole is a connector and an orchestrator of capability to get things done – the right things. A typical day in the life of Nicole sees her turn her hand to consulting, speaking, writing, judging, mentoring and managing complex programs of work.

She works on the front line of innovation bringing organizations kicking and screaming into the 21st Century

The Work

- Getting to the root cause and then helping teams deliver the aims and ambitions of their plans and strategies. This is across all sizes of projects and campaigns.
- From a large enterprise, to mid-size and niche businesses , THE NYC brings its vast network of skills. This means it can act as a leverage where needed and bring the correct skills and capacity.
- Nicole is also an advisor to all sizes and shapes of businesses. She helps them manage them through their own disruptions to developing their own innovation capacity and creating new offerings for clients.

The Tools

The NYC host, take part, develop workshops and deliver all kinds of advice and content to drive innovation into its clients.

The NYC leverages its network. It brings unlimited capability to all kinds of programs of work. It prides itself on orchestration and choreography in execution across all sectors to solve the challenges of the 21st Century.

Printed in Great Britain
by Amazon

42044258R00152